TEMPTAT

TEMPTATION

VÁCLAV HAVEL

Translated by George Theiner

faber and faber
LONDON · BOSTON

First published in 1988
by Faber and Faber Limited
3 Queen Square London WC1N 3AU
Reprinted in 1990

Printed in England by Clays Ltd, St Ives plc
All rights reserved

This translation of *Temptation* first appeared in
Index on Censorship in November/December 1986.

British Library Cataloguing in Publication Data

Havel, Václav
Temptation.
I. Title
891.8′625   PG5038.H3/

ISBN 0–571–15105–1

For Zdeněk Urbánek

CHARACTERS

DR HENRY FOUSTKA, *scientist*
FISTULA, *invalid in retirement*
The DIRECTOR
VILMA, *scientist*
The DEPUTY DIRECTOR
MAGGIE, *secretary*
DR LIBUŠE LORENCOVÁ, *scientist*
DR VILÉM KOTRLÝ, *scientist*
DR ALOIS NEUWIRTH, *scientist*
MRS HOUBOVÁ, *Foustka's landlady*
DANCER (*male*)
PETRUŠKA
SECRETARY
FIRST LOVER
SECOND LOVER

Before the curtain rises, in the intervals between the scenes, and during the Intermission, we hear 'cosmic' or 'astral' rock music. It is important for the intervals to be as short as possible – thus the scene changes (despite the variety of settings) carried out as quickly as possible.

Temptation was first performed at The Other Place,
Stratford-upon-Avon, on 22 April 1987.

The cast was as follows:

DR KOTRLÝ	Ian Barritt
FISTULA	David Bradley
DR LORENCOVÁ	Susan Colverd
MAGGIE	Sally George
VILMA	Julie Legrand
DR NEUWIRTH	Trevor Martin
DEPUTY DIRECTOR	Barrie Rutter
DR FOUSTKA	John Shrapnel
DIRECTOR	Paul Webster

Director	Roger Michell
Set Design	David Roger
Costumes	Alexandra Byrne
Music	Jeremy Sams
Lighting	Rick Fisher

SCENE ONE

We are in one of the rooms of a scientific institute. It combines the functions of an office, consulting-room, library, staff room, and foyer. There are three doors, at the rear, at the front left and front right. At right rear there is a bench, a small table and two chairs; against the rear wall stands a bookcase, a couch, and a white vitrine filled with drugs and various exhibits such as embryos, models of human organs, cult objects of primitive nations, and so on. At left is a desk with a typewriter and papers on it, behind it an office chair, and by the wall a filing cabinet. A large chandelier hangs in the middle of the room. There can also be other objects – a wash-basin, a sun lamp, and so on. The furnishings do not testify to any specific interest, much less any particular personality – rather, they reflect the undefined character of the Institute itself. The whole gives the impression of bureaucratic anonymity, the individual objects having found their way here thanks to the arbitrary decisions of someone in authority rather than because they were actually needed. As the curtain rises, we see LORENCOVÁ, KOTRLÝ *and* NEUWIRTH. LORENCOVÁ *is wearing a white coat and is sitting at the desk, powdering her face, her powder compact propped against the typewriter.* KOTRLÝ, *also in a white coat, is stretched out on the bench, reading a newspaper.* NEUWIRTH, *in ordinary clothes, is standing by the bookcase, his back to the others, examining one of the books.*

A short pause.

LORENCOVÁ: (*Calling*) Maggie . . .

    (MAGGIE *enters, left.*)

MAGGIE: Yes, Doctor.

LORENCOVÁ: Oh, Maggie, would you make me a cup of coffee?

MAGGIE: Yes, of course.

KOTRLÝ: (*Without looking up*) And one for me, please.

NEUWIRTH: (*Without turning round*) And me . . .

MAGGIE: That's three coffees, then?

LORENCOVÁ: Right.

    (MAGGIE *leaves, left. A short pause, then* FOUSTKA *enters quickly by the rear door. He is wearing a black sweater and black trousers, carries a briefcase, is slightly out of breath.*)

I

FOUSTKA: Hi . . .

KOTRLÝ: (*Lays aside his newspaper*) Hi, Henry.

NEUWIRTH: (*Puts away his book and turns round*) Hi there . . .

(LORENCOVÁ *puts her mirror and powder compact in her coat pocket and crosses to the bench to join* KOTRLÝ, *thus vacating the desk for* FOUSTKA. *He puts down his briefcase and hastily removes some papers from it, watched intently by the others.*)

FOUSTKA: Have they been yet?

KOTRLÝ: Not yet.

LORENCOVÁ: Where's Vilma?

FOUSTKA: Oh, she's slipped out to get some oranges.

(MAGGIE *enters left, carrying three cups of coffee on a small tray; two she places on the table in front of* LORENCOVÁ *and* KOTRLÝ, *handing the third to* NEUWIRTH, *still standing at the back, leaning against the bookcase.*)

LORENCOVÁ: Thanks very much.

(MAGGIE *returns to the door, left.*)

FOUSTKA: Oh, Maggie . . .

MAGGIE: (*Stops*) Yes, Doctor?

FOUSTKA: Sorry about this, but would you mind making another cup of coffee for me?

MAGGIE: Of course not.

FOUSTKA: Thanks.

(MAGGIE *leaves, left.* LORENCOVÁ, KOTRLÝ *and* NEUWIRTH *stir their coffee, at the same time keeping their eyes on* FOUSTKA, *who has taken his place behind the desk and is tidying up various papers and files on it. The lengthy, tense silence is at last broken by* KOTRLÝ.)

KOTRLÝ: (*To* FOUSTKA) Well . . . ?

FOUSTKA: Well what?

KOTRLÝ: How goes it?

FOUSTKA: What, exactly?

(LORENCOVÁ, KOTRLÝ *and* NEUWIRTH *look at one another and smile. A short pause.*)

LORENCOVÁ: Why, your private studies, of course.

FOUSTKA: I don't know what you're talking about.

(LORENCOVÁ, KOTRLÝ *and* NEUWIRTH *look at one another and smile. A short pause.*)

NEUWIRTH: Oh, come off it, Henry – every little child here knows about it.

FOUSTKA: I don't give a damn what little children know about – I am engaged in no other studies than those pertaining directly to my work here at the Institute.

KOTRLÝ: I know what it is – you don't trust us, do you? Can't say I blame you . . . in certain matters caution is called for.

NEUWIRTH: Especially if one is engaged on two fronts at once . . .

FOUSTKA: (*Giving* NEUWIRTH *a quick glance.*)
And what's that supposed to mean?
(NEUWIRTH *points a conspiratorial finger, first round the room and then at the door, right, indicating the power of the Institute, then he points at the ceiling and at the floor, indicating the power of Heaven and Hell.*)
You're all letting your imaginations run away with you. What about that social tonight – is it still on?

LORENCOVÁ: Naturally . . .
(*The* DEPUTY DIRECTOR *enters, right, in his ordinary clothes, accompanied by* PETRUŠKA *who is wearing a white coat. They are holding hands, as they will throughout, which means that* PETRUŠKA, *who will not say a word, will invariably accompany the* DEPUTY. *He, however, pays no attention to her, as if he were merely taking her along as some kind of personal effect or mascot.* LORENCOVÁ, KOTRLÝ *and* NEUWIRTH *rise.*)

KOTRLÝ: Good morning, sir.

DEPUTY: Good morning, friends. Sit down, sit down, please, you know that neither I nor the Director like to stand on ceremony.
(LORENCOVÁ, KOTRLÝ, *and* NEUWIRTH *sit down again. A short pause.*)
So what's the news? Did you all sleep well? Any problems? I don't see Vilma here . . .

FOUSTKA: She phoned to say her bus had broken down. But she had managed to find a taxi, she said, so she should be here any minute . . .
(*Short pause.*)

3

DEPUTY: Looking forward to the social, are we? I hope you're all coming?

KOTRLÝ: I'm coming, definitely . . .

LORENCOVÁ: We're all coming.

DEPUTY: Excellent! Personally, I consider our social evenings to be a splendid idea – splendid. Particularly as regards their collectively therapeutic effect. Remarkable how quickly and effectively they help to solve the various interpersonal problems which crop up among us from time to time. Simply thanks to the way we, as individuals, invariably loosen up, while, as a collective, we somehow grow stronger. Wouldn't you say?

KOTRLÝ: Yes, quite, that's exactly how I see it.

DEPUTY: Quite apart from the fact that it would be criminal not to make at least occasional use of such a fine garden.
(*A pause.*)
I came a little earlier on purpose . . .

NEUWIRTH: Is something wrong?

DEPUTY: The Director will tell you himself. All I wanted was to ask you to be sensible – do try to understand him and don't make unnecessary problems for him, he is in a difficult enough position as it is. We all know, after all, that you can't knock down a brick wall with your bare hands – so why make things needlessly difficult for yourselves or for others? I think we can be glad we have such a Director, so that if we lend him support, we're really doing ourselves a favour. Let us bear in mind that he is concerned for our common cause, and that he is no more his own master than the rest of us. It is therefore up to us to display at least a minimum of self-discipline so that neither he, our Institute, nor any one of us should get into hot water. I'm sure you understand and won't expect me to say more than I've already said and am able to say. We're all adults, after all, are we not?

KOTRLÝ: Yes, of course.

DEPUTY: There you are, then. Have you had your soap ration?

FOUSTKA: They're due to bring it today.

DEPUTY: Excellent!

(*The* DIRECTOR *enters, right, wearing a white coat.*
LORENCOVÁ, KOTRLÝ *and* FOUSTKA *rise quickly.*)

KOTRLÝ: Good morning, Director.

DIRECTOR: Hullo there, friends. Do sit down, please, you
know that I don't like to stand on ceremony.

DEPUTY: That's just what I told our colleagues, just now,
Director.

(LORENCOVÁ, KOTRLÝ *and* FOUSTKA *sit down. The*
DIRECTOR *gazes at all those present inquisitively, then goes to*
FOUSTKA *and holds out his hand to him.* FOUSTKA *gets up,
surprised.*)

DIRECTOR: (*To* FOUSTKA) Did you sleep well?

FOUSTKA: Yes, thank you.

DIRECTOR: Do you have any problems?

FOUSTKA: No, I don't think so . . .

(*The* DIRECTOR *squeezes* FOUSTKA's *elbow in a friendly
fashion and turns to the others.* FOUSTKA *sits down again.*)

DIRECTOR: Where is Vilma?

DEPUTY: She phoned to say her bus had broken down. But she
had managed to find a taxi, she said, so she should be here
any minute . . .

(MAGGIE *enters, left, with a cup of coffee, which she gives to*
FOUSTKA.)

FOUSTKA: Thanks.

MAGGIE: Don't mention it.

(MAGGIE *leaves, left.*)

DIRECTOR: Looking forward to the social, are we?

KOTRLÝ: Very much, Director.

DEPUTY: I have good news for you, friends. The Director has
promised to make a short appearance at our social.

LORENCOVÁ: A short one?

DIRECTOR: That'll depend on the circumstances. (*To* FOUSTKA)
I hope you'll show up?

FOUSTKA: Yes, of course, Director.

DIRECTOR: Look here, colleagues, no sense in making a meal of
it. We all have work to do. So let me get straight to the
point: as you probably know, there have lately cropped up
complaints that our Institute isn't fulfilling its tasks in

5

keeping with the present situation . . .

NEUWIRTH: What situation?

DIRECTOR: Come, come, my friend, let's not beat about the bush. Are we not the people who're supposed to be the first to know things, and the first to take action? But to continue: we're being urged, with increasing insistence, that we go over to the offensive, that is that we should at last somehow try and implement a programme of extensive educational, popular-scientific and individually therapeutic activity . . .

DEPUTY: Firmly in the spirit of the scientific *Weltanschauung* . . .

DIRECTOR: That, surely, goes without saying?

DEPUTY: I'm sorry, Director, but unfortunately there exists science that is not based on a scientific view of the world . . .

DIRECTOR: That is no science where I'm concerned! Now, where was I?

KOTRLÝ: You were saying that we must somehow try and implement . . .

DIRECTOR: Yes. In order to counter the isolated but nevertheless alarming expressions of various irrational viewpoints which can be discerned in particular in certain members of our younger generation and which owe their origin to the incorrect . . .

The SECRETARY *enters, right. He goes to the* DIRECTOR *and at length whispers in his ear, the* DIRECTOR *nodding all the time and looking serious. The* SECRETARY *stops whispering, the* DIRECTOR *nods for the last time, the* SECRETARY *leaves, right. A short pause.*)

Now, where was I?

KOTRLÝ: You were saying that the irrational viewpoints we have to counter owe their origin . . .

DIRECTOR: To the incorrect interpretation of the complexity of natural processes and the historical dynamism of human civilization, some of whose aspects are taken out of context, only to be interpreted, either in the light of pseudo-scientific theories . . .

DEPUTY: We have discovered that type-written copies of some of the works of C. J. Jung are circulating among our young people . . .

DIRECTOR: Or in the light of a whole range of mystic prejudices, superstitions, obscure teachings and practices spread by certain charlatans, psychopaths and members of the intelligentsia . . .

(VILMA *comes running in through the rear door. She seems breathless and is carrying a bag of oranges.*)

VILMA: Sorry to be late, Director, but just imagine – the bus I was on . . .

DIRECTOR: Yes, I've heard. Sit down.

(VILMA *sits down on the couch, gesticulating at* FOUSTKA *and obviously trying to convey some message to him.*)

Look here, colleagues, no sense in making a meal of it. We all have work to do. I have already acquainted you with the size of the problem and the tasks it puts in front of us. Now it is up to you. All I want to do is to ask you to be sensible, try and understand and don't make unnecessary problems for me in what is a difficult enough position as it is. We live in modern times, after all.

KOTRLÝ: Yes, that's right, we do.

DIRECTOR: There you are, then. Have you had your soap ration?

FOUSTKA: They're due to bring it today.

(*The* DIRECTOR *goes to* FOUSTKA, *who rises. The* DIRECTOR *puts his hand on* FOUSTKA's *shoulder and looks him gravely in the face. Then, in a voice charged with emotion, he says:*)

DIRECTOR: I rely on you, Henry . . .

FOUSTKA: You mean, where the soap is concerned?

DIRECTOR: The soap and everything else.

(*Curtain.*)

SCENE TWO

Foustka's flat. A small bachelor's room with a single door at rear right. The walls are covered by bookcases with large quantities of

7

*books; a window, left, and in front of it a large writing desk covered
with papers and yet more books, with a chair behind it and a low
couch to the right. Next to this, a large globe, while on one of the
bookcases hangs a map of the heavens. As the curtain rises,*
FOUSTKA *is discovered kneeling in the middle of the room, in a
dressing-gown, with four burning candles on the floor around him.
He holds a fifth in his left hand, and a piece of chalk in his right,
with which he draws a circle round himself and the candles. Next to
him on the floor lies an open old tome. The room is dimly lit. When*
FOUSTKA *has finished drawing his circle he studies the book for a
time, then shakes his head and murmurs something. There is a knock
on the door.* FOUSTKA, *startled, jumps up and calls out.*

FOUSTKA: (*Calling*) Just a moment.
  (FOUSTKA *quickly switches on the light, puts out all the
  candles, which he hides behind the desk, removes the book,
  looks around and with his foot tries to obliterate the circle he has
  drawn on the floor.*)
  (*Calling*) Who is it?

HOUBOVÁ: (*Off stage*) It's only me, Doctor.

FOUSTKA: (*Calling*) Just a minute, Mrs Houbová.
  (*Clears room.*) Come in.

HOUBOVÁ: Oh dear, the place is full of smoke. You need some
  air.

FOUSTKA: It really doesn't bother me. Anything wrong?

HOUBOVÁ: You have a visitor . . .

FOUSTKA: Have I? Who is it?

HOUBOVÁ: I don't know, he didn't tell me.

FOUSTKA: A stranger, is it?

HOUBOVÁ: Never seen him before.

FOUSTKA: What does he look like?

HOUBOVÁ: I dunno – how should I say, a bit disreputable . . .
  and, worst of all, he . . .

FOUSTKA: What is it, Mrs Houbová?

HOUBOVÁ: I hardly like to say . . .

FOUSTKA: Go on, out with it . . .

HOUBOVÁ: Well, it's just that he . . . smells . . .

FOUSTKA: Is that so? How does he smell?

HOUBOVÁ: Hard to say – like a strong cheese, I guess.

8

FOUSTKA: Does he really! Never mind, tell him to come in.

(HOUBOVÁ *leaves the room, leaving the door ajar.*)

HOUBOVÁ: (*Off stage*) You're to go in ...

(FISTULA *enters, a small, slender man with a limp and of dubious appearance. He is holding a paper bag containing a pair of slippers.* HOUBOVÁ *stands in the doorway, following him with her eyes, then shrugs her shoulders at* FOUSTKA *and shuts the door.* FISTULA *grins vacuously.* FOUSTKA *regards him with some astonishment. A pause.*)

FOUSTKA: Good afternoon.

FISTULA: How do you do?

(*A pause.* FISTULA *inspects the room with interest.*)

Very cosy, very cosy indeed. Just as I imagined it. All these learned books ... a rare globe ... everything nice and restrained ... balance in all its glory.

FOUSTKA: Balance? What balance? And anyway, who am I speaking to?

FISTULA: All in good time. May I sit down?

FOUSTKA: Please do ...

(FISTULA *sits down on the couch, takes off his shoes, removes his slippers from the paper bag and puts them on, replacing them with the shoes and laying the bag on the couch next to him. A pause.*)

FISTULA: I take it I don't have to stress that you should not mention my visit to anyone in your own interest as well as mine?

FOUSTKA: Why should I not mention it?

FISTULA: You'll see soon enough. My name is Fistula. My place of work is immaterial – in any case I don't have a permanent job. Don't have to, you see, being retired as an invalid.

(FISTULA *grins as if he had made a joke.*)

FOUSTKA: I'd hazard a guess that you work in a cheese factory.

(FISTULA *laughs, then grows serious.*)

FOUSTKA: Athlete's foot, my dear sir, or some similar ailment I suffer from, and there's little I can do about it.

(FOUSTKA *perches himself on a corner of the desk and stares at* FISTULA, *with a mixture of curiosity, suspicion and revulsion.*

9

A longer pause.)
Aren't you going to ask me what it is I want? What is the purpose of my visit?

FOUSTKA: Well, I have not yet given up the hope that you will tell me without being asked.

FISTULA: Of course, there is nothing to prevent me doing just that, and if I haven't done so already, then for a very good reason.

FOUSTKA: What reason is that?

FISTULA: I had rather hoped you'd discover that for yourself.

FOUSTKA: (*Irritated*) How can I when I see you for the first time? And anyway, I have neither the time nor the inclination to play silly guessing games. Unlike you, I happen to have a job and will shortly have to go ...

FISTULA: I know, to your Institute's social. You have bags of time.

FOUSTKA: How did you know I'm going to our social?

FISTULA: And before I arrived you didn't exactly carry on like a man in a hurry.

FOUSTKA: You can't know anything about what I was doing before you arrived.

FISTULA: Forgive me, but I know far more than you about what I know and what I don't know, and how I know what I know.

(FISTULA *gives another of his asinine grins. A longer pause. Then* FOUSTKA *gets up from the table, walks around it to stand facing* FISTULA, *a serious expression on his face.*)

FOUSTKA: Look here, Mr ...

FISTULA: Fistula ...

FOUSTKA: Mr Fistula, I'm asking you straight, and I expect a straight answer: what is it you want?

(*A short pause.*)

FISTULA: Does the name Marbuel mean anything to you? Or Loradiel? Or Lafiel?

(FOUSTKA *looks startled, but recovers his composure, looks at* FISTULA *and shouts.*)

FOUSTKA: Out!

FISTULA: I beg your pardon?

FOUSTKA: I said: Out!

FISTULA: How do you mean – out?

FOUSTKA: Leave my flat at once and never show your face here again.

(FISTULA *rubs his hands together contentedly*.)

Did you hear what I said?

FISTULA: Yes, I heard what you said, and I'm delighted at your reaction because it confirms that I have come to the right address . . .

FOUSTKA: I don't understand . . .

FISTULA: Your agitation tells me that you're well aware of the weight of my contacts, which you would hardly be in a position to know unless you had earlier taken an interest in them yourself.

FOUSTKA: Those names mean nothing to me, I have no idea what you're talking about, and the suddenness of my decision to throw you out is due simply to the fact that I have suddenly had enough of you. It is mere coincidence that this happened just as you pronounced those names. Having provided this explanation, perhaps I can repeat what I said earlier without fear that you will put some false interpretation on it: leave my flat at once and never show your face here again!

FISTULA: Your first request – that I leave – I'll naturally comply with, even though not just yet; the second I will not, and you will in time be very grateful to me for it.

FOUSTKA: I'm afraid you didn't understand. Those weren't two mutually independent requests – in fact, they weren't requests at all. It was a command, single and indivisible.

FISTULA: Understood. However, I must add, the alacrity with which you subsequently attributed a different motive to that command, together with the circumstance that, although you had, to use your expression 'had enough of me', you nevertheless found it necessary to acquaint me with this, thus running the risk of postponing my desired departure – all this proves just one thing: that your original fear of me as a representative of those contacts has given way to a fear of me as a possible *agent provocateur*. I therefore have to tell you that this, too, I anticipated. Nay, what is more, if this had not happened I should have found it suspicious and would have had to ask myself if indeed *you* are not an *agent provocateur*. But now let's get down to the matter in hand. There is of course no way I can *prove* to you that I am no *provocateur*; even were I to call forth Ariel himself, here and now, it would not exclude the possibility that I am also trying to provoke you. You thus have only three choices: you can continue to consider me an *agent provocateur* and insist that I leave. Secondly, not to think of me in those terms but instead to trust me. Thirdly, not to make your mind up in this matter just yet and to adopt a waiting posture, which means not to throw me out but on the other hand to say nothing which, if I were an *agent provocateur*, I might be able to use against you. If I may, I'd recommend the third alternative . . .

(FOUSTKA *paces up and down the room in thought, then he sits behind his desk and looks at* FISTULA.)

FOUSTKA: All right, so be it. I should add, though, that in talking to you, I have no need to watch what I say because there is no question that I might think, much less utter, anything that could be used against me.

FISTULA: Splendid! (*He claps enthusiastically.*) I like you. If I were an *agent provocateur*, I'd have to admit that you have passed your first test with flying colours. Your words betray a well-founded caution as well as a sharp intelligence and ready wit, all of which are qualities I can but welcome, for they give me hope that I can rely on you and that we shall work well together . . .

(*A pause.*)

FOUSTKA: Now, listen here, Mr . . .

FISTULA: Fistula . . .

FOUSTKA: Listen here, Mr Fistula, I'd just like to say two things. Firstly: to my mind you talk too much and I wish you'd come more quickly to the point and tell me what brought you here. You have given me no indication, even though I asked you for a straight answer to my straight question. And secondly: it comes as something of a surprise to me to hear that you and I are supposed to be working together on anything. It takes two to tango, you know.

FISTULA: You have just used eighty-seven words to reply to me. Considering their semantic value, that is not exactly a small number, so I would not accuse others of talking too much if I were you.

FOUSTKA: Loquaciousness is well known to be infectious . . .

FISTULA: I hope that in time you will also acquire some of my more important skills.

FOUSTKA: What's that? Are you trying to tell me you want to teach me things?

FISTULA: Not just teach . . .

FOUSTKA: No? What else, for God's sake?

FISTULA: (Shouts) Leave him out of this!

FOUSTKA: What else do you have in mind, then?

FISTULA: (Smiling) To initiate you . . .

(FOUSTKA rises abruptly, bangs the desk with his fist, and shouts.)

FOUSTKA: That's enough! I am a scientist and hold a scientific world view, working in a very responsible position in one of our foremost scientific institutes. If anyone comes to me with ideas that can be defined as an attempt to spread superstition, I shall be forced to act according to my scientific conscience.

(FISTULA stares dumbly at FOUSTKA for a few seconds, then starts to laugh uproariously, hopping about the room as he does so. Suddenly he falls silent, bends down, and slowly draws a circle with his finger on the floor, just as FOUSTKA had done earlier. Then he leaps to his feet and again bursts out laughing. Crossing to the desk, he seizes one of the hidden candles, waves it in the air and, still laughing, places it on the desk. FOUSTKA follows his antics with a glazed look in his eyes. FISTULA suddenly grows serious again, returns to the couch, sits down, and begins to speak in level tones.)

FISTULA: Doctor, I am well acquainted with your views, I know how much your work at the Institute means to you, so please accept my apologies for my stupid joke. In any case, it's high time I abandoned these introductory pleasantries. As your Director was good enough to stress this morning, one of the tasks facing your Institute is to combat certain expressions of irrational mysticism, which still crop up here and there, kept alive by obscure individuals as the remnants of the pre-scientific views of primitive nations and dark historical epochs. As a scientist, you yourself know best that this struggle of yours will be the more effective, the more thorough your knowledge of that which you are struggling against. You have in your possession a remarkable collection of hermetic literature – just about everything worth having, from Agrippa and Nostradamus to Eliphas Levi and Papus – but as you well know, theory is not everything, and I'd seriously doubt that you have never felt the urge to acquaint yourself directly with contemporary magical practice. I come to you as a practitioner with several hundred successful magical evocations behind him, who is prepared to acquaint you with some aspects of his work in order to provide valuable material for your scientific studies. And if you are asking yourself how it is possible for a hermetic to take an interest in the struggle against hermetism, I can give you a frank answer: I find myself in a situation where, without some support, I might come to a sticky end. I therefore offer myself to you as a subject for study, and I shall ask for nothing more in return than that you should, if necessary, testify that I have put myself at the disposal of science and that it would thus be unfair to hold me responsible for spreading something that I am, in actual fact, helping to combat.

(FISTULA *looks gravely at* FOUSTKA, *who is lost in thought for a while. Then he speaks softly.*)

FOUSTKA: I have a suggestion . . .

FISTULA: Yes? I'm listening . . .

FOUSTKA: In order to expedite matters, I'll pretend not to be equipped with a scientific world view, as if I were taking an interest in certain things out of mere curiosity.

FISTULA: Agreed!

(FISTULA *comes forward and holds out his hand to* FOUSTKA.

FOUSTKA *hesitates, then takes his hand and shakes it.*
FOUSTKA *swiftly withdraws his hand again.*)
FOUSTKA: (*Cries out*) Ouch!
(FOUSTKA *rubs his hand and waves it in the air, his face
distorted with pain.*)
Man, your temperature must be fifty below!
FISTULA: (*Laughs*) Not quite . . .
(FOUSTKA *at last recovers and resumes his seat at his desk.*
FISTULA *also sits down, crossing his hands in his lap and
gazing at* FOUSTKA *in a theatrical manner. A longer pause.*)
FOUSTKA: Well?
(*A long pause.*)
What is it?
(*A long pause.*)
Lost your tongue all of a sudden?
FISTULA: I'm waiting . . .
FOUSTKA: Waiting for what?
FISTULA: Your wishes.
FOUSTKA: I don't understand – what wishes?
FISTULA: How can I acquaint you with my knowledge unless
you set me certain tasks – such as you can yourself verify?
FOUSTKA: Oh, I see. What kind of tasks do you have in mind –
roughly?
FISTULA: Come, you know enough about these things . . .
FOUSTKA: Yes, perhaps, but faced with this opportunity of a
practical demonstration . . .
FISTULA: No matter, I'll help you. How about this for an
innocent first step. As far as I know, you fancy a certain
young lady . . .
FOUSTKA: I don't know what you're talking about . . .
FISTULA: Oh come, Doctor, after all that has been said here,
surely you cannot doubt that I might be privy to a secret or
two . . .
FOUSTKA: If you mean the secretary at the Institute, I don't
deny that she is pretty, but that hardly entitles you . . .
FISTULA: What if tonight at that social of yours she were to fall
in love with you? Unexpectedly and, of course, just for a
short time? How about that?

(FOUSTKA *paces the room nervously then turns sharply to*
FISTULA.)

FOUSTKA: Please go away!

FISTULA: Who? Me? Why?

FOUSTKA: Yes, you. Go away.

FISTULA: You're not starting that again? Just when I thought
we had come to an understanding.

FOUSTKA: You have insulted me . . .

FISTULA: Insulted you? How?

FOUSTKA: Do you think I'm so badly off that I have to use
magic to help me with women? I'm not some dirty old man
conducting experiments on unsuspecting innocent young
virgins for his own sexual gratification. What do you take
me for?

FISTULA: None of us really knows what we're capable of. But
that's not the point. If my well-meant, innocent, spur-of-
the-moment little idea offends you in any way, I naturally
apologize and withdraw it.

FOUSTKA: And another thing: I have a girl-friend and I am
faithful to her.

FISTULA: As she is to you?

FOUSTKA: (*Startled*) Yes. What are you saying?

FISTULA: Forget it . . .

FOUSTKA: No, just a minute – you can't get away with hints
like that. I'm not interested in gossip.

FISTULA: Sorry I spoke. If you have decided to turn a blind
eye, that is entirely your business . . .
(FISTULA *removes his shoes from the paper bag and slowly puts
them on.* FOUSTKA *looks on in some embarrassment. A pause.*)

FOUSTKA: Are you leaving?
(*A pause.*)
I just let off a little steam . . .
(*A pause.* FISTULA *has changed his footwear, put his slippers
back in the paper bag, and is slowly making his way to the
door.*)
So what's to become of it?

FISTULA: (*Stops and turns*) What's to become of what?

FOUSTKA: Our agreement, I mean.

16

FISTULA: Well . . ?
FOUSTKA: Is it still on?
FISTULA: That is entirely up to you.
  (FISTULA *grins. The curtain falls.*)

SCENE THREE

The garden of the Institute. It is night, and the garden is illuminated with Chinese lanterns suspended from wires among the trees. In the middle there is a small summer-house, behind it a space serving as a dance-floor. Front left, a garden bench, right, a garden table with various drinks and glasses. All around are trees and shrubs, which combine with the dim light to screen the dancers from view; figures moving about the garden are also seen only dimly. Only the action at front of the stage can be clearly seen. As the curtain rises, the music grows softer and changes in character: we hear commercial dance music, which will accompany the entire scene. Two LOVERS *are sitting in the summer-house; they will remain there throughout the scene, gently embracing, stroking and kissing each other and whispering in each other's ear, oblivious to their surroundings. The* DEPUTY *is dancing with* PETRUŠKA *and* KOTRLÝ *with* LORENCOVÁ; *apart from these two couples, the* DIRECTOR *and* VILMA *move around the dance-floor separately.* FOUSTKA *is standing by the refreshments table, pouring two drinks;* MAGGIE *is sitting on the bench. Everyone is in evening dress, the ladies in formal gowns. As the scene opens,* FOUSTKA *is explaining something to* MAGGIE, *who listens in rapt silence. As he speaks,* FOUSTKA *finishes pouring the drinks and walks slowly over to* MAGGIE, *carrying the two glasses.*

FOUSTKA: We have to realize that out of the infinite number of
    possible velocities, the expansion of the universe chose
    precisely the one which gave rise to the universe as we
    know it, that is, with sufficient time and other prerequisites
    for the formation of solid bodies, so that life could exist on
    them – or at least on one of them! Isn't that a remarkable
    coincidence?
MAGGIE: Yes, quite remarkable.

(FOUSTKA *has now reached* MAGGIE *and hands her one of the glasses, sits down next to her, and they both sip their drink.*)

FOUSTKA: It is, isn't it. And if you delve further, you'll discover that you owe your existence to such an incredible number of equally incredible coincidences that it exceeds all conceivable ratios of probability. Surely all this cannot be an accident; behind it must be concealed some more profound intention of existence, of the world and of nature, willing you, me to exist, willing life as such to exist, and at its apex, as far as it is given to us at present to know, the human spirit capable of reflecting on all this. Does it not strike you as if the cosmos had actually determined to see itself one day through our eyes and to put the questions which we are now putting, with our lips?

MAGGIE: Oh yes, that's exactly how it strikes me.

(VILMA, *who has left the dance-floor, appears at the table, and pours herself a drink.*)

VILMA: Having a good time, you two?

FOUSTKA: Maggie and I have been discussing some philosophical questions . . .

VILMA: Oh, in that case, don't let me disturb you . . .

(VILMA, *glass in hand, disappears; a little later she can again be seen dancing solo on the dance-floor.*)

FOUSTKA: And another thing: modern biology has long been aware that while the law of the survival of the fittest and similar discoveries explain a great deal, they fail altogether to explain why life should exist in the first place, life with the endless variety of its manifestations, life, which seems to be here only because existence wishes to display its own power. But for whose sake, though? Have you ever given any thought to this?

MAGGIE: Not quite like that, I must admit. But now, I guess I'll think about it always . . . you know how to put it so nicely.

(NEUWIRTH *appears from the right, comes up to the bench, and bows to* MAGGIE.)

NEUWIRTH: May I have the pleasure?

MAGGIE: (*Embarrassed*) Why . . . yes . . . of course . . .

(MAGGIE *gives* FOUSTKA *a questioning, unhappy look, then gets up.*)

FOUSTKA: You'll come back, won't you?

MAGGIE: But of course! It's all so terribly interesting . . .

(NEUWIRTH *offers his arm to* MAGGIE *and the two disappear, to be seen again a little later, dancing.* FOUSTKA, *lost in thought, sips his drink. The* DIRECTOR, *who has left the dance-floor, appears from behind a shrub to the left of the bench.*)

DIRECTOR: A splendid evening, isn't it?

(FOUSTKA, *startled, gets up.*)

FOUSTKA: Why, yes . . . we've been lucky in the weather . . .

DIRECTOR: Do sit down. May I join you?

FOUSTKA: Yes, please do . . .

(*They both sit down on the bench. A slight pause. Then the* DIRECTOR *takes* FOUSTKA *by the hand and looks closely into his eyes.*)

DIRECTOR: Henry . . .

FOUSTKA: Yes . . . ?

DIRECTOR: Tell me frankly – what do you think of me?

FOUSTKA: What . . . do I think . . . ? Well, how should I say, I think that everyone at the Institute is glad that you are in charge . . .

DIRECTOR: No, you don't understand. What I want to know is what you personally think of me – as a man . . . or, to put it more accurately, what are your feelings towards me?

FOUSTKA: I feel great respect for you . . .

DIRECTOR: Respect. Is that all?

FOUSTKA: Well . . . how to say it . . . it's very difficult . . .

(*The* DEPUTY DIRECTOR *appears on the right, accompanied by* PETRUŠKA, *having left the dance-floor; they are holding hands. The* DIRECTOR *sees them and lets go of* FOUSTKA's *hand, to* FOUSTKA's *evident relief.*)

DEPUTY: So here you are, Director. We've been looking for you . . .

DIRECTOR: Anything wrong?

(*Taking advantage of the situation,* FOUSTKA *gets up and quickly walks away.*)

DEPUTY: Nothing in particular. It's only that Petruška here wants to ask you something but is too shy to say so . . .

DIRECTOR: Ask me what?

DEPUTY: She wants to ask you whether you would dance with her.

DIRECTOR: I'm afraid I don't know how to lead, I'd only trample her dress. But there are so many better dancers here . . .

DEPUTY: In that case, would you at least accept our invitation and accompany us to the pond, where colleague Kotrlý has built a delightful underwater light display.

(*The* DIRECTOR *gets up, irritated, and goes off to the right with the* DEPUTY *and* PETRUŠKA. *At the same time,* KOTRLÝ *and* LORENCOVÁ *appear on the left, having left the dance-floor. They cross to the refreshments table.*)

KOTRLÝ: Have you seen my underwater light display yet?

LORENCOVÁ: You're doing it all wrong, Willy.

KOTRLÝ: What am I doing wrong?

(*They have reached the table and* KOTRLÝ *pours two drinks, handing one to* LORENCOVÁ. *They both sip their drinks.*)

LORENCOVÁ: You're crawling so abjectly that before long those two idiots will get fed up with you and you'll be the laughing stock of the Institute. Apart from which, everyone will want to see you come a cropper.

KOTRLÝ: Maybe I *am* doing it all wrong, but that's still better than pretending I'm not interested and at the same time telling 'em everything . . .

LORENCOVÁ: I take it you're referring to Neuwirth?

KOTRLÝ: Who else? Who was it first started blabbing about Foustka's dabbling in magic? If they get to hear of it, Neuwirth will be to blame.

LORENCOVÁ: But we all talked about it! You're being unfair to Neuwirth; your only excuse is that you're jealous . . .

KOTRLÝ: I might have known you'd take his side!

LORENCOVÁ: Look, don't start that again!

KOTRLÝ: Líba, give me your word there is nothing between you.

LORENCOVÁ: I give you my word. How about another dance?

(KOTRLÝ and LORENCOVÁ *put down their glasses and go off
to the right; a little later they can be seen dancing in the
background.* NEUWIRTH *and* MAGGIE *appear from the left.*
MAGGIE *sits down on the bench,* NEUWIRTH *remains
standing. From behind the bench* FOUSTKA *pops up round a
shrub and sits down next to* MAGGIE.)

NEUWIRTH: Oh, well, let me not disturb you ...
(NEUWIRTH *goes off, to be seen a little later dancing with*
LORENCOVÁ, *whom he has taken away from* KOTRLÝ. *Also
on the dance-floor can now be seen the* DEPUTY *dancing with*
PETRUŠKA, *and the* DIRECTOR, *dancing on his own. A short
pause.*)

MAGGIE: Go on, talk some more! Each word of yours seems to
open my eyes ... I can't understand how I could have been
so blind – so superficial ...

FOUSTKA: I'd just like to start, if I may, from a completely
different angle. Have you ever thought that we would be
quite unable to understand even the most simple moral
action which is not motivated by self-interest, that in fact it
would appear to be quite absurd, if we did not admit to
ourselves that somewhere within it there is concealed the
prerequisite of something higher, some absolute,
omniscient and infinitely just moral authority, through
which and in which all our actions gain a mysterious worth
and through which each and every one of us constantly
touches eternity?

MAGGIE: Yes, yes, that's exactly how I've always felt it to be.
Only I was never able to say it, let alone put it into such
splendid words.

FOUSTKA: There you are! All the more tragic, then, that
modern man has chosen to deny everything that is larger
than him, to deride the very notion that there might be
something higher and that his life and the world at large
could possibly have some higher meaning. Having set
himself up as the highest authority, he now watches in
horror where the world is heading.

MAGGIE: Isn't it all so clear and simple! I do admire the way
you look at these things in such a ... well, I mean, it's all

so original . . . so different from the way people usually talk
about them . . . and you take it all so seriously. I don't
think I'll ever forget this evening. I feel as if, in your
company, I'm becoming a new person every minute –
please don't be annoyed that I'm being so frank, but you
seem to emanate a . . . I don't understand how I could have
been indifferent to you all this time . . . in a word, I've
never felt anything like this before.

(KOTRLÝ *appears from the right, approaches the bench, and
bows to* MAGGIE.)

KOTRLÝ: May I have the pleasure?

MAGGIE: Oh, I'm sorry, but . . .

KOTRLÝ: Oh, come on, Maggie – we haven't danced together
yet.

(MAGGIE *gives* FOUSTKA *an unhappy look; he just shrugs his
shoulders;* MAGGIE *gets up.*)

MAGGIE: (*To* FOUSTKA) You'll wait here for me, won't you?

FOUSTKA: Yes, of course.

(KOTRLÝ *offers his arm to* MAGGIE *and the two disappear, to
be seen again a little later, dancing.* FOUSTKA, *lost in thought,
sips his drink. The* DIRECTOR, *who has left the dance-floor,
appears from behind a shrub to the left of the bench.*)

DIRECTOR: Alone again, are you?

(FOUSTKA, *startled, gets up.*)

Sit down, Henry, sit down . . .

(FOUSTKA *resumes his seat. The* DIRECTOR *again takes*
FOUSTKA *by the hand and looks closely into his eyes.*)

DIRECTOR: Henry . . . ?

FOUSTKA: Yes?

DIRECTOR: Would you like to be my deputy?

FOUSTKA: Your deputy? Me?

DIRECTOR: I could swing it . . .

FOUSTKA: But you already have a deputy . . .

DIRECTOR: If only you knew how I loathe that shit.

(*The* SECRETARY *enters, right. He goes to the* DIRECTOR *and
whispers at length in his ear, the* DIRECTOR *nodding all the
time and looking serious. The* SECRETARY *stops whispering,
the* DIRECTOR *nods for the last time, the* SECRETARY *leaves,*

right. The DIRECTOR, *who has clung to* FOUSTKA's *hand all this time, now turns to* FOUSTKA *and stares long and hard into his eyes.*)

DIRECTOR: Henry ...

FOUSTKA: Yes?

DIRECTOR: How about coming back to my place when this is over? Or we needn't stay till the end, simply disappear. I have some home-made cherry brandy and I'd show you my collection of miniatures, and we could have a good chat, undisturbed. If it got late, and you didn't feel like making your way home, you could stay the night. You know that I live all alone, and it's only a stone's throw from the Institute, so you'd find it easy in the morning ... What do you say?

FOUSTKA: Thank you very much, I appreciate your invitation, but you see, I've already promised ...

DIRECTOR: Who? Vilma?

(FOUSTKA *nods. The* DIRECTOR *again looks him straight in the eye, then irritably pushes his hand away, jumps up, crosses to the refreshments table, pours himself a drink and downs it in a single gulp.* FOUSTKA *remains sitting on the bench, not quite knowing what to do. The* DEPUTY *and* PETRUŠKA, *who have left the dance-floor, appear on the left; they are holding hands and make straight for the* DIRECTOR.)

DEPUTY: So here you are, Director. We've been looking for you ...

DIRECTOR: Anything wrong?

DEPUTY: Nothing in particular. Petruška and I just wanted to ask you what you're doing after this is over. We should be honoured if you'd accept our invitation for a nightcap. Of course, you can sleep at our place, should you wish ...

DIRECTOR: No, I'm sorry, I am very tired. I have to go home ...

(*The* DIRECTOR *marches off to the right. The* DEPUTY *follows him with his eyes, then disappears, left, abashed and with* PETRUŠKA *in tow. A little later they can be seen dancing in the background. At the same time,* NEUWIRTH *and* LORENCOVÁ *appear, right, having left the dance-floor.*)

NEUWIRTH: I've seen a lot, but the sight of an educated man trying to curry favour with his cretinous bosses with tricks such as those coloured electric bulbs in the bloody pond – that really takes the biscuit!

(NEUWIRTH *pours two drinks, handing one to* LORENCOVÁ. *They both sip their drinks.*)

LORENCOVÁ: I'd say it's better to curry favour with those coloured bulbs in the pond than to pretend you're not interested and at the same time tell 'em everything . . .

NEUWIRTH: I might have known you'd take his side!

LORENCOVÁ: Look, don't start that again!

NEUWIRTH: Líba, give me your word there is nothing between you.

LORENCOVÁ: I give you my word. How about another dance?

(NEUWIRTH *and* LORENCOVÁ *put down their glasses and go off to the left; a little later they can be seen dancing in the background.* KOTRLÝ *and* MAGGIE *appear from the right.* MAGGIE *sits down on the bench next to* FOUSTKA. KOTRLÝ *remains standing. An embarrassed pause.*)

KOTRLÝ: Oh, well, don't let me disturb you . . .

(KOTRLÝ *goes off, to be seen a little later dancing with* LORENCOVÁ, *whom he has taken away from* NEUWIRTH.)

FOUSTKA: When man drives God out of his heart, he makes way for the Devil. What else is this contemporary world of ours, with its blind, power-crazed rulers and its blind, powerless subjects, what else is the catastrophe that is being prepared under the banner of science – with us as its grotesque flag-bearers – what else is it other than the work of the Devil? It is well known that the Devil is a master of disguise. Can you imagine a more ingenious disguise than that offered him by our modern lack of faith? No doubt he finds he can work best where people have stopped believing in him. Forgive me for speaking so frankly, Maggie, but I cannot hold it back any longer. But who else can I confide in but you?

(MAGGIE *throws her glass into the bushes, grasps both* FOUSTKA's *hands, and cries:*)

MAGGIE: I love you!

FOUSTKA: No!

MAGGIE: Yes, and I'll go on loving you till the day I die.

FOUSTKA: You unhappy girl! With me you're doomed.

MAGGIE: Rather doomed with you and in truth, than to live
without you and live a lie.

(MAGGIE *embraces* FOUSTKA *and begins to kiss him
passionately,* VILMA *appears by the side of the refreshments
table, having left the dance-floor. For a while she gazes at the
kissing couple, then she says in an icy voice.*)

VILMA: Having a good time?

(FOUSTKA *and* MAGGIE *jump apart and look at* VILMA *in
consternation. The curtain falls.*)

SCENE FOUR

VILMA's *flat. It is a comfortable place, furnished like a lady's
boudoir, full of antique furniture. A door at rear; on the left a large
bed with a canopy; on the right, two armchairs, a large Venetian
mirror, and a dressing-table with a multitude of jars and perfume
bottles. The room is full of scattered knick-knacks and woman's
clothes, only* FOUSTKA's *evening dress lies neatly folded by the bed.
Evident care has been taken to match the colours in the apartment,
with pink and violet predominating. As the curtain rises,* FOUSTKA
is sitting in his underpants on the edge of the bed, VILMA, *wearing a
lace negligée, by the dressing-table, facing the mirror and with her
back to* FOUSTKA. *She is combing her hair. A short pause.*

FOUSTKA: When was he here last?

VILMA: Who?

FOUSTKA: Oh, don't ask such stupid questions!

VILMA: You mean that dancer? About a week ago . . .

FOUSTKA: And you let him in?

VILMA: He just brought me a bunch of violets. I told him I
didn't have time, that I was meeting you . . .

FOUSTKA: I asked whether you let him in.

VILMA: I don't remember . . . maybe he did come in for a
while . . .

FOUSTKA: So you kissed each other.

25

VILMA: I kissed him on the cheek when he gave me those violets. That's all.

FOUSTKA: Vilma, be so kind as not to treat me like an idiot. A kiss on the cheek! Once you let him in I'm sure he'd expect a little more than that. At the very least he'd want to dance with you.

VILMA: Henry, please leave it alone. Can't you find something more interesting to talk about?

FOUSTKA: Did he or didn't he?

VILMA: All right, if you must know, he did. And that's all I'm going to say. I refuse to discuss this any longer because it's undignified, offensive and ridiculous. As if you didn't know that I love you and that no dancer can pose a threat to you. So please no more of this interrogation. After all, I don't give *you* the third degree – even though I have more reason to than you.

FOUSTKA: So you refuse to answer? That, of course, speaks for itself.

VILMA: I have told you again and again that he means nothing to me, I don't go out of my way to see him, I don't dance with him. What more am I supposed to do, damn it?

FOUSTKA: He's always flitting around you, flattering you, wanting to dance with you – and you lap it up! If you didn't, you'd have put an end to it long ago.

VILMA: All right. I don't deny his attentions flatter me. Any woman would feel the same. I'm touched by his persistence, the way he refuses to give up even though he knows he hasn't got a chance. Would you be capable of turning up here at night, from heaven knows where, just to hand me a bunch of violets – at the same time knowing it was hopeless?

FOUSTKA: He persists because you deny him in a way that kindles his hope, and you resist him in a fashion that fuels his desire. If only you'd slam the door on those hopes of his, he'd never show his face here again. But you won't do that because it amuses you to play cat-and-mouse with him. You whore!

VILMA: You have obviously made up your mind to insult me.

FOUSTKA: For how long did you dance with him?

VILMA: Now that's really enough, Henry. You're becoming a bore. I've known for a long time that you're something of an eccentric, but I'd never have guessed you could be so vicious. You seem to be in the grip of a pathological jealousy. And you're being insensitive, tactless, petty-minded and vengeful to boot! If at least you had a real reason . . .

FOUSTKA: So you intend to go on whoring?

VILMA: You have no right to speak to me like this! You spent the whole evening dancing attendance on that stupid girl, embarrassing everybody in sight, while I trotted around like an idiot – and now you start reproaching *me*. Me! You do as you bloody well please and I have to suffer in silence – and we end up with you making a scene on account of some stupid dancer. How ridiculous can you get! Do you realize how unjust it all is? Do you understand how selfish and cruel you've become?

FOUSTKA: First of all, I don't dance attendance on anybody, and I won't have you referring to Maggie as 'that stupid girl'; secondly, we're not talking about me now, we're talking about you, so kindly don't try to change the subject. Sometimes it seems to me that there is some monstrous plot behind all this: you first of all arouse feelings in me which I had thought long since dead, and then – having robbed me of my ability to be objective about things – you spin your treacherous web around my heart, the more vile since it is woven out of a large number of threads of seemingly innocent dancing visits. Well, I'm not going to let myself be stretched on this rack any longer. I'm going to do something to myself . . . or him . . . or you – or all of us!

(VILMA *lays down her comb, rises, and advances smilingly towards* FOUSTKA, *clapping her hands as she does so.*
FOUSTKA *now also smiles and goes forward to meet her.*)

VILMA: Your performance gets better every day.

FOUSTKA: Well, you're pretty good yourself . . .

(FOUSTKA *and* VILMA *embrace each other tenderly, kiss, then walk slowly towards the bed. They sit up in it next to each*

27

other, lean back against the pillows, and cover their legs with a
duvet. FOUSTKA *lights a cigarette for both of them. A longish*
pause is broken by VILMA.)

VILMA: Tell me, Henry –

FOUSTKA: Yes?

VILMA: Don't you get tired of it at times?

FOUSTKA: Tired of what?

VILMA: Of me making you take part in these games?

FOUSTKA: Well, truth to tell, it did irritate me at first.

VILMA: And now?

FOUSTKA: Now it's beginning to scare me.

VILMA: *Scare* you? Why is that?

FOUSTKA: It seems to me I'm beginning to take it a bit
seriously.

VILMA: (*Cries out*) Henry! You're not really getting jealous, are
you? That's wonderful. I never thought such a success
possible. That you would show anything but a *feigned*
jealousy . . .

FOUSTKA: Sorry, but I can't share your enthusiasm . . .

VILMA: I don't see what it is you're afraid of.

FOUSTKA: Of myself.

VILMA: Oh, come on.

FOUSTKA: No, don't underestimate it, Vilma. Something is
going on inside me – I feel I'd be capable of doing things
that were always alien to me. As if something that had lain
hidden deep inside me was suddenly floating to the surface.

VILMA: You do exaggerate, Henry. For once you feel a little
healthy jealousy, and you're panicking. There's nothing the
matter with you; maybe you're a little disconcerted by the
goings on at the Institute, after tonight's unfortunate
encounter with the Director – no, don't deny it, it *is*
worrying you even if you don't want to admit it – but it's
getting at you sub-consciously, and you then see bogeys
where there aren't any.

FOUSTKA: If only it were as simple as that . . .
(*A pause.*)

VILMA: You think he'll destroy you?

FOUSTKA: He'll certainly try. Question is, does he have the

necessary power?

VILMA: He has as much power as he wants – certainly where we're concerned.

FOUSTKA: But there are other kinds of power than that which he happens to wield.

(VILMA *jumps up in bed, startled, and kneels on a pillow facing* FOUSTKA.)

VILMA: You're serious, aren't you?

FOUSTKA: Yes.

VILMA: Now you are scaring *me*. Please promise me you won't dabble in anything of that sort.

FOUSTKA: What if I don't promise?

VILMA: I told you that invalid would bring us nothing but trouble. He's got you all confused. Don't tell me you would really take him up on his offer?

FOUSTKA: Well, why not?

VILMA: That's dreadful!

FOUSTKA: At least you can see I wasn't just letting off steam.

(*The doorbell rings,* VILMA *cries out, and quickly hides under the bedclothes.* FOUSTKA *smiles, gets up just as he is, in his underpants, crosses to the door and opens it. The* DANCER *is standing in the doorway, with a bunch of violets hidden behind his back.*)

DANCER: Good evening. Is Vilma in?

FOUSTKA: Why?

DANCER: (*Shows him the flowers*) I just wanted to give her something . . .

FOUSTKA: (*Calls in the direction of the bed*) Vilma, you've got a visitor . . .

(VILMA *climbs out of bed, a little confused; she can't find anything to put on, so she finally goes to the door in her negligée.* FOUSTKA *moves aside but stays where he is.*)

VILMA: Thank you . . .

DANCER: Well, I'll be off again . . . sorry if I disturbed you . . .

VILMA: Bye-bye then.

(*The* DANCER *leaves;* VILMA *shuts the door, smiles uncertainly at* FOUSTKA, *lays the violets down on a table, comes up to* FOUSTKA *and kisses him gently on the forehead, cheeks and mouth.* FOUSTKA *stands as if rooted to the spot, gazing coldly in front of him.*)

I love you.

(FOUSTKA *does not bat an eyelid, as* VILMA *goes on kissing him. Then suddenly* FOUSTKA *slaps her brutally across the face;* VILMA *falls to the ground;* FOUSTKA *kicks her. The curtain falls.*)

SCENE FIVE

The same room in the Institute as that in which Scene One took place. As the curtain rises the room is empty, but then FOUSTKA *and* VILMA *enter by the rear door.* FOUSTKA *is still wearing the evening clothes he had on the previous night;* VILMA *a white coat. She has a black eye. They both seem happy.*

VILMA: Don't tell me we're the first!

FOUSTKA: Have you noticed that you only arrive on time when I sleep at your place?

VILMA: You do exaggerate . . .

(FOUSTKA *sits down at the desk and arranges the papers on it;* VILMA *sits down on the couch.*)

(*Calls out*) Maggie . . .

(MAGGIE *enters by the door left, dressed in office clothes. When she catches sight of* FOUSTKA *she stops and lowers her eyes.*)

Would you make us two coffees? Strong ones, if possible.

MAGGIE: Yes, yes, of course . . .

(MAGGIE *returns nervously to the door, stealing a glance at* FOUSTKA *as she goes. He looks up from his papers and gives her a jovial smile.*)

FOUSTKA: Did you sleep well?

MAGGIE: (*Stammering*) Yes, thank you, well . . . why no, not really . . . I had so much to think about . . .

(MAGGIE *leaves the room in obvious confusion.*)

VILMA: I'd say, Henry, that you really managed to turn the poor girl's head last night.

FOUSTKA: Oh, she'll get over it.

(*A pause.*)

VILMA: Henry . . .

FOUSTKA: Yes, darling?

VILMA: It was good last night, wasn't it? I can't remember when we made love so beautifully . . .

FOUSTKA: Mmm.

(LORENCOVÁ *enters by the rear door, in ordinary clothes, accompanied by* KOTRLÝ, *also in civvies, and* NEUWIRTH *wearing a white coat.*)

KOTRLÝ: Oh, you're here already.

VILMA: Surprised, aren't you?

(LORENCOVÁ *and* KOTRLÝ *take their places on the bench,* NEUWIRTH *leans against the bookcase.*)

LORENCOVÁ: (*Noticing* VILMA's *black eye*) What on earth is that?

VILMA: Unbridled passion, what else?

(MAGGIE *enters, left, carrying two cups of coffee on a tray. She hands one to* VILMA *and places the other with a shaking hand in front of* FOUSTKA.)

FOUSTKA: Thank you.

LORENCOVÁ: How about us, Maggie . . .

MAGGIE: Yes, of course, Doctor . . .

(MAGGIE *departs quickly, left. The* DEPUTY *enters, right, in a white coat and with* PETRUŠKA *in a dress; they are holding hands. The others get up.*)

KOTRLÝ: Good morning, sir.

DEPUTY: Good morning, friends. Sit down, sit down. I see that today you're all here early. Splendid, though today of all days I'd hardly have expected it.

(*They all sit down again.*)

Well, I believe we had a most successful evening last night. You all deserve thanks for that. Of course, special recognition goes to Kotrlý here for his underwater lighting effects.

KOTRLÝ: Oh, that was nothing . . .

DEPUTY: No point, friends, in beating about the bush . . .

NEUWIRTH: Anything wrong?

DEPUTY: The Director will tell you himself. All I wanted was to ask you to see things as they are, and to try and help us as we try to help you, and in particular that you keep a cool head at this difficult juncture – a cool head, a passionate heart and clean hands. There are moments in life when people either show their mettle – in which case they have nothing to fear – or they don't measure up – and then they have only themselves to thank for the unnecessary difficulties they create for themselves. But you're all educated people, and so I don't have to draw you a picture, do I? Now, who'll volunteer to clear up the garden?

KOTRLÝ: I will, if you like. I have to remove all those bulbs anyway.

DEPUTY: Splendid.

(*The* DIRECTOR *enters, right, in ordinary clothes. They all get up again.*)

KOTRLÝ: Good morning, Director.

DIRECTOR: Good morning, friends. I see that today you're all here early. Splendid, though today of all days I'd hardly have expected it, and yet it is particularly important this morning . . .

DEPUTY: That's just what I told our colleagues just now, Director.

(*They all sit down again. The* DIRECTOR *looks at them for a while, studying their faces, then he goes to* KOTRLÝ *and holds out his hand to him.* KOTRLÝ *gets up, surprised.*)

DIRECTOR: (*To* KOTRLÝ) Did you sleep well?

KOTRLÝ: Yes, thank you.

DIRECTOR: Do you have any problems?

KOTRLÝ: No, I don't think so . . .

(*The* DIRECTOR *squeezes* KOTRLÝ*'s elbow in a friendly fashion and turns to the others.* KOTRLÝ *sits down again.*)

DIRECTOR: Look here, colleagues, no sense in making a meal of it . . .

NEUWIRTH: Anything wrong?

DIRECTOR: As we all know, our Institute is a kind of lighthouse of true knowledge, indeed, I might say it is – in its role of a vigilant guardian of the very scientific nature of science – something like the avant-garde of progress. One could say, to put it in a nutshell: what we think today, others will live tomorrow!

DEPUTY: Yes, Director, I have already reminded our colleagues of the responsibility this role places on all of us . . .

DIRECTOR: But why am I telling you all this . . . Something serious has happened.

(*The* SECRETARY *enters, right. He goes to the* DIRECTOR *and whispers at length in his ear, the* DIRECTOR *nodding all the time and looking serious. The* SECRETARY *stops whispering, the* DIRECTOR *nods for the last time and resumes speaking; the* SECRETARY *leaves, right.*)

But why am I telling you all this. Something serious has happened.

(MAGGIE *enters, left, carrying three cups of coffee on a small tray; two she places on the table in front of* LORENCOVÁ *and* KOTRLÝ, *handing the third to* NEUWIRTH. *Then she crosses to the same door, left.*)

But why am I telling you all this . . . Something serious has happened.

(MAGGIE *stops in the doorway, looks at the* DIRECTOR, *then at* FOUSTKA, *and then stays by the door, listening.*)

NEUWIRTH: Anything wrong?

DEPUTY: (*To* NEUWIRTH) Please don't interrupt the Director. He's just about to tell us . . .

DIRECTOR: Something serious has happened. The virus has lodged where one would least have expected it, but where, at the same time, it can cause the most damage – that is, in the very centre of the anti-virus campaign – or, to stay with the metaphor – in the central store of antibiotics.

(*All those present look at one another in consternation.* VILMA *and* FOUSTKA *exchange glances showing that they know what it is all about;* FOUSTKA *nervously tries to find a cigarette, takes one out and lights it.*)

KOTRLÝ: Are you telling us, Director, that right here – someone – that one of us . . .

DIRECTOR: Yes, that's exactly what I am telling you, filled as I am with deep sorrow, shame and indignation. We have here in our midst, in this scientific institute – I underline the word scientific – someone who for a long time now and of course in complete secrecy, which only goes to show his two-faced character, has been engaged in various so-called hermetic practices, beginning with astrology, through alchemy all the way to magic, seeking in these murky waters the hidden treasure of allegedly higher – in other words, pre-scientific – learning.

KOTRLÝ: Does that mean he believes in ghosts?

DIRECTOR: Not only that – he has been trying to combine theory with practice. We have ascertained that he has established contact . . .

LORENCOVÁ: With spirits?

DIRECTOR: That's enough! Kindly do not jest about matters that are a blot on the work of our Institute, a direct attack on its reputation and thus a blow below the belt to all of us, and in particular to me who carries the responsibility for our scientific credibility. This is a very grave and sad matter, my friends, and it is up to us all to find an honourable solution. Where was I?

DEPUTY: You were speaking about those contacts . . .

DIRECTOR: Oh yes. Recently, as we have ascertained, he made contact with a certain element from the murky world of pseudo-science, common criminality and moral degeneration, who is suspected of spreading superstition and fooling credulous people with his tricks, and who moreover dabbles in such poisonous things as satanism, black magic, and similar heinous practices. That then is how things stand, and I throw the meeting open to discussion. Any questions?

(*A heavy pause. Then* KOTRLÝ *speaks out softly.*)

KOTRLÝ: May we know the name of this . . . colleague?

DIRECTOR: (*To the* DEPUTY) Tell them.

DEPUTY: I can scarcely bring myself to say it, but name him I must. Very well then – it is Dr Foustka.

(*A heavy pause.*)

DIRECTOR: Yes; anyone else wish to speak?

MAGGIE: (*Diffidently*) Yes, I do . . .

FOUSTKA: (*To* MAGGIE) No – please stay out of this!

DIRECTOR: This concerns us all without exception.

MAGGIE: Forgive me, Director, I am no scientist and I don't

know how to put it – but this simply can't be true! Dr Foustka is a wise and honourable man . . . I know he is . . . he worries about things which by rights we all should be worrying about – he tries to think things out for himself . . . to get to the bottom of things . . . all the important things, that is, the sources of morality, the order of the universe . . . All the rest – all this talk about those contacts . . . I simply don't believe it. I'm sure it's all just gossip, put about by malicious people who wish to harm him. (*There follows a deathly silence.* FOUSTKA *is obviously desperately unhappy at* MAGGIE's *intervention. The* DIRECTOR *turns to the* DEPUTY.)

DIRECTOR: (*To the* DEPUTY) When we finish here, please arrange for her immediate dismissal. Our Institute really cannot now afford the luxury of employing secretaries who accuse the management of lying.

DEPUTY: I'll see to it, Director.

DIRECTOR: (*To* MAGGIE) You can go and pack your things . . .

FOUSTKA: (*Softly, to* MAGGIE) What possessed you? So needlessly to ruin your life – who'll give you a job after this?

MAGGIE: I want to suffer with you!

FOUSTKA: Excuse me, Director, would it not be more sensible to send her for treatment? You can see she doesn't know what she is saying.

DIRECTOR: Psychiatric hospitals are not a cloakroom where one deposits girls whom one first confuses with high-falutin ideas and then wants to get rid of . . .

MAGGIE: Are you renouncing me, Henry? And renouncing everything you told me last night?

FOUSTKA: (*Angrily, through clenched teeth*) Be quiet, do you hear?
(MAGGIE *bursts into tears and runs out, left. An embarrassed pause.*)

VILMA: (*To* FOUSTKA) If she does something foolish, it'll be your fault.

FOUSTKA: (*To* VILMA) You'd like that, wouldn't you?

VILMA: (*Softly*) Don't start . . .

35

FOUSTKA: (*Softly*) Who's starting? Me?

DIRECTOR: Quiet, please. I'll enquire upstairs whether she might not be able to take a job as a cleaner with one of the housing administrations.

LORENCOVÁ: That would be a sensible and humane solution . . .

DIRECTOR: (*To* FOUSTKA) Do you wish to make use of your right to respond to the accusation that has been made against you?

(FOUSTKA *gets up slowly and leans against the desk as if it were a lectern.*)

FOUSTKA: Director, Deputy Director, colleagues. I am confident that my case will be dealt with fairly and objectively, and I assume therefore that when the time comes I shall be given the opportunity to give a more detailed explanation and that some of the circumstances I shall be able to elucidate will lead to my complete vindication. For the time being, however, I shall confine myself to expressing the hope that the investigation will, in keeping with our scientific approach to reality and our scientific morality, be unprejudiced and have the one and only aim of uncovering the truth. Not only in my interest and in the interest of science, which it is the task of our Institute to protect and cultivate, but also in the interests of you all: otherwise my case could easily become merely the first link in a long chain of injustice with consequences I dare not even contemplate. Thank you for your attention.

(FOUSTKA *sits down. An embarrassed pause: they are all uneasy, though each for a different reason.*)

DIRECTOR: We are living in modern times and no one here has the slightest intention of staging a witch-hunt. That would only be to revive the old ignorance and fanaticism, against which we are fighting. Let the manner in which Dr Foustka's case is handled become a model of a truly scientific approach to facts, which will provide inspiration for us all. Truth must prevail, whoever suffers in the process.

(*A short pause.*)

Who has volunteered to tidy up the garden?

KOTRLÝ: I did, Director.

(*The* DIRECTOR *goes to* KOTRLÝ, *who rises. The* DIRECTOR *puts his hand on* KOTRLÝ's *shoulder and looks him gravely in the face. Then, in a voice charged with emotion, he says:*)

DIRECTOR: I am delighted that you have taken on this task, Vilém. I shall come and give you a hand.

(MAGGIE *enters, left, dressed in ordinary clothes and carrying a small suitcase. She has been crying, and crosses the room as if in a trance, leaving by the rear door. As she closes it, the chandelier falls down. It hits no one but smashes into little pieces on the floor. The curtain falls.*)

(*Intermission*)

SCENE SIX

FOUSTKA's *flat. Only* FISTULA *is on stage as the curtain rises. He is sitting behind the desk, examining the papers lying on it. He is wearing slippers, the paper bag containing his shoes is on top of the desk among all the papers.* FOUSTKA, *still wearing his evening clothes, enters. He is startled to find* FISTULA *sitting there.*

FOUSTKA: (*Cries out*) What the . . . what're you doing here?

FISTULA: Waiting for you.

FOUSTKA: How did you get in?

FISTULA: No, not down the chimney, if that's what you're worried about. I came in through the door, which Mrs Houbová kindly opened for me before she went off to do her shopping. You see, I explained to her that you urgently wanted to speak to me and that, given my gammy leg, I could hardly be expected to wait outside on the pavement.

FOUSTKA: You mean you lied – as usual . . .

FISTULA: Don't you believe I'm an invalid?

FOUSTKA: You lied when you pretended that I was anxious to see you. The truth is, on the contrary, that after everything that's happened, I was hoping never to clap eyes on you again.

37

FISTULA: On the contrary, what has happened makes our meetings that much more desirable.

FOUSTKA: Be all that as it may – how dare you rummage among my papers?

FISTULA: Well, I had to find something to do while I waited . . .

FOUSTKA: And what about those shoes?

FISTULA: Oh, come now, don't be such an old fusspot . . .

(FISTULA *gives one of his asinine grins, then picks up the paper bag, goes over to the couch and sits down, depositing the bag next to him.*)

Why don't you sit down?

(FOUSTKA, *still angry, crosses to the desk, sits down and looks at* FISTULA.)

Well, what do you say – pretty successful so far, wouldn't you agree?

FOUSTKA: Successful? What might you be referring to?

FISTULA: I'd never have expected you to manage it so quickly and so easily. You're a good learner, I must say.

FOUSTKA: I haven't the slightest idea what you're talking about.

FISTULA: Oh yes, you have. Did we not agree first of all to carry out a little innocent experiment? And it succeeded beyond all expectation, don't you think?

FOUSTKA: If you mean that that wretched child developed a crush on me, let me just tell you two things: first and foremost, that was no work of magic, much less your doing.

All that happened was that I had . . .

FISTULA: Quite by chance . . .

FOUSTKA: Quite by chance, an opportunity to talk to her properly for the first time, and that, as it happens . . .

FISTULA: By chance . . .

FOUSTKA: . . . I was on form that night, so that she found what I had to say interesting. Well, as such girls do, her interest soon switched . . .

FISTULA: By chance . . .

FOUSTKA: . . . from the topic of conversation to the speaker. I can't see anything out of the ordinary in that. And, secondly: seeing what consequences this event had for the girl, I bitterly regret that it ever happened, even though I had no idea – how could I? – that our innocent talk would *have* such consequences . . .

(FISTULA *laughs uproariously, banging his thighs with his hands.*)

Would you mind telling me what's so funny?

FISTULA: (*Grows serious*) My dear Doctor! We all know that you don't believe in such unscientific things as mere chance and the workings of coincidence. You have obviously not asked yourself how it was that you, who up till then were just about capable of requesting her to make you a cup of coffee, were suddenly waxing so eloquently in front of the girl, courageously spouting ideas which you well knew could put your career at the Institute in jeopardy. Does it not seem odd to you that this should have happened just when we had hatched our little scheme? And does it not surprise you that your ideas alone – as if someone had waved a magic wand – overcame all the girl's inhibitions, kindling a love that nothing can destroy?

FOUSTKA: Oh, we all have our moments when we somehow manage to transcend ourselves . . .

FISTULA: Yes, that's just it! That is what I'm talking about!

FOUSTKA: I don't understand . . .

FISTULA: You surely didn't think that the spirit of love, Jeviel, would turn up and arrange everything for you like some mundane matchmaker? How else do you think he could fix it except through you yourself? It's quite simple, really – he, so to speak, took over your body. Or rather, he aroused and liberated something in you that's always been there but had lain dormant until then.

FOUSTKA: You don't say!

FISTULA: The human mind, after all, is not an inert mass – you must know that better than I do, being a scientist. If the seed is to sprout, someone has first to sow it . . .

FOUSTKA: If – I say *if* – you and your . . . whatever-his-name-is . . .

FISTULA: Jeviel . . .

39

FOUSTKA: If you and your Jeviel *are* in any way responsible for sowing that seed, then I curse the two of you from the bottom of my heart. You're a devil and I don't want to have anything more to do with you.

FISTULA: Why are you being so dense? If the devil exists, then he is within all of us . . .

FOUSTKA: In that case you must be his favourite abode.

FISTULA: You overestimate me, my dear sir, in just the same way as a moment ago you overestimated yourself. I am no more than a catalyst, helping my fellow men to bring out something that exists in them without my intervention. It is just that with my assistance they then find in themselves the courage to lead a more exciting life, to enjoy life to the full and to be more truly themselves. We only live once, so why should we spend those few decades that are allotted to us stifling under the gag of life-denying scruples? You know why you called me a devil? To rid yourself of responsibility – and to ease your conscience by, as the scientists say, 'transferring' or 'projecting' it on to me. I do hope that you will succeed in outwitting your scruples in this way. But you must understand that I – an insignificant invalid – could not budge you by so much as an inch if you did not *want* to be budged, if indeed you had not dreamed about being budged long ago. Our little experiment was merely designed to bring these trivialities home to you.

FOUSTKA: In that case what was all that about its being so innocent? A barefaced lie!

FISTULA: Wrong again! You are once more only trying to lie to yourself. You could easily have told the girl how infallible was the scientific view of the world, you could have expounded on the world-shattering importance of the work your Institute is doing, and she would have been quite safe. And even having chosen the other course, you still didn't have to abandon her so selfishly when it came to the crunch. But that's not the point. I really have to compliment you on one thing – that, for a beginner, you acquitted yourself really well. Your disguise in the saintly habit of an impassioned seeker after (*He points a finger at the*

40

ceiling.) as the true source of the meaning of the universe and of all moral imperatives – that was truly magnificent! I take my hat off to you.

FOUSTKA: (*Angrily*) What disguise? I was saying exactly what I believed to be true.

FISTULA: My dear friend . . .

FOUSTKA: I am no friend of yours!

FISTULA: My dear sir, truth is not merely what we are thinking, but also why, to whom and under what circumstances we say it.

(FOUSTKA *gazes fixedly at* FISTULA *for a few moments, then sadly nods, strides up and down the room a few times, and sits down again. After a short pause he says in a quiet voice:*)

FOUSTKA: I don't know how they managed it, but somehow they've found out that I have had contact with you, and as a result it is highly likely that I'll be fired, made an example of, publicly disgraced, and no doubt completely destroyed. The reason why all this is about to happen to me is – at least where I'm concerned – immaterial. I see the true meaning of my downfall in something else. It will be a just punishment for my unforgivable irresponsibility, for my having succumbed to temptation, under the influence of a poisonous, unsubstantiated, evil jealousy which my over-weening pride caused to grow within me. Thus I tried to kill two birds with one stone, to gain the affections of one and to hurt another. Yes, I was blinded by some devilish impulse in my heart, and I must therefore be grateful to you for helping me realize this – whatever your motives or methods. By awakening both the temptation and the jealousy, you enabled me to see myself from the darker side. Not only that: your explanation has thrown light on the true source of my error, which as you rightly say has to be sought inside me and nowhere else. I therefore do not regret our meeting – if that's the word for the way you insinuated yourself into my life. I have learned an important lesson, and your dark intentions have served to illuminate my own behaviour. I am telling you all this because – I sincerely hope and believe – this is the last time

41

I shall see you. And that you will leave now, this very
minute.

(*A long pause.* FISTULA *slowly extracts his shoes from the
paper bag, looks at them thoughtfully, smells them, then at last
puts them down on the floor in front of him and turns, smiling,
to* FOUSTKA.)

FISTULA: We are engineers of our own fate. I was going to say
something, but now I'm not sure that it wouldn't be better
to wait until you are – if I may so put it – a little more
receptive . . .

FOUSTKA: No, go on, what did you want to say?

FISTULA: I am as well acquainted with the thought processes
you have just been kind enough to demonstrate for me as I
am with these old shoes of mine. We hermetics call it the
Smíchovský Compensation Syndrome.

FOUSTKA: And what's that when it's at home?

FISTULA: Whenever a beginner successfully breaks the carapace
of his or her earlier inhibitions, thus giving free passage to
all one's latent possibilities, there follows the inevitable
'hangover', accompanied by a bout of what I can only call
masochistic self-accusation and self-chastisement.
Psychologically speaking, this is a perfectly natural
reaction. In his desire to, so to speak, belatedly mollify his
scruples, principles, whatever, the person concerned re-
interprets the action by means of which he betrayed them
so that it becomes a kind of purifying act, a lesson he has
had to learn in order to become a better human being. In
short, he turns it into a sort of little dance-floor on which to
perform the ritual celebration of his principles. Usually it
doesn't take long before he sobers up and comes to realize
something that we of course are well aware of but cannot
explain to him: I mean the grotesque discrepancy between
the worthlessness of the scruples in whose name he
demanded the direst punishment for himself, and the
fundamental value of the experience which he was trying
thus to expiate . . .

(FOUSTKA *jumps up and bangs the desk in fury.*)

FOUSTKA: All right – that's it! If you think for a minute that by your speechifying you're going to inveigle me into some dubious adventure, you're bloody well mistaken!

FISTULA: No, my dear sir, it is you who are mistaken if you fondly believe that you're *not* inveigled already . . .

FOUSTKA: (*Shouts*) Get out!

FISTULA: May I just point out that when you return to reality and, who knows, feel like consulting me, I may not be there to be consulted. However, that is your funeral . . .

FOUSTKA: Just piss off, would you. If it's all right with you, I'd like to be left alone with my Smíchovský Compensation Syndrome.

(FISTULA *slowly picks up his shoes, shaking his head as he does so. Then he throws the shoes on the floor, jumps to his feet and starts to pound his forehead with his hand.*)

FISTULA: I don't believe this! Driven by her unreasoning jealousy because he had the audacity to spend a few minutes in a philosophical discussion with another woman, his mistress shops him to his superiors and tells them he has had contacts with a magician . . .

FOUSTKA: What are you suggesting?

FISTULA: And he would be willing to let them deprive him of his job, his scientific career, perhaps his entire property! Without so much as lifting a finger in his own defence. Well, I've seen a lot in my time but this is something else! Even old Smíchovský himself would have a fit if he heard this!

FOUSTKA: I simply do not believe that Vilma could do something like that. After all the sunny moments of pure happiness we've known together!

FISTULA: That just goes to show how little you know women. It may well be the memory of those sunny moments that provided the motive force for her action.

(FISTULA *calms down, resumes his seat, and slowly removes his slippers. He smells them and then carefully replaces them in the paper bag, then puts on his shoes. A long pause.*)

FOUSTKA: (*Softly*) Well, what would you suggest I do?

FISTULA: Oh, forget it . . .

FOUSTKA: Surely you can tell me?

43

FISTULA: You should have realized by now that I don't go around dispensing advice or fixing things. At most I'll occasionally provide someone with a stimulus . . .

(*Having put his shoes on,* FISTULA *picks up the paper bag and makes for the door.*)

FOUSTKA: (*Shouts*) Don't talk in riddles, damn you!

(FISTULA *stops, stands stock still for a few moments, then turns round to face* FOUSTKA.)

FISTULA: All you have to do is to summon up, in a good cause, at least a small fraction of the cunning which your dear Director makes use of, in pursuance of wicked causes, from morning till night.

(FISTULA *starts to grin;* FOUSTKA *stares at him in some consternation; the curtain falls.*)

SCENE SEVEN

The same room in the Institute in which Scenes One and Five took place. A naked bulb, suspended by a wire, hangs in place of the chandelier. As the curtain goes up, LORENCOVÁ, KOTRLÝ *and* NEUWIRTH *are on stage.* LORENCOVÁ, *wearing a white coat, is sitting behind the desk, powdering her face, her powder compact propped against the typewriter.* KOTRLÝ, *also in a white coat, is stretched out on the bench, reading a newspaper.* NEUWIRTH, *in ordinary clothes, is standing by the bookcase, his back to the others, examining one of the books. A short pause.*

LORENCOVÁ: Who's now going to make us coffee?

KOTRLÝ: (*Without looking up*) Why don't you go and make it?

LORENCOVÁ: Why don't *you*?

(FOUSTKA *enters quickly by the rear door. He is wearing a black sweater and black trousers, carries a briefcase, is slightly out of breath.*)

FOUSTKA: Hi . . .

NEUWIRTH: (*Without turning round*) Hi.

(*The others do not acknowledge* FOUSTKA's *arrival, each carrying on with what he or she was doing.* FOUSTKA *stands his briefcase on top of the desk and hurriedly extracts some papers from it.*)

FOUSTKA: Have they been yet?

NEUWIRTH: (*Without turning round*) Not yet.

(*When* FOUSTKA *realizes that* LORENCOVÁ *will not vacate the desk for him, he crosses to the bench and sits down next to* KOTRLÝ. *A pause.*)

LORENCOVÁ: Poor Maggie . . .

(FOUSTKA *looks up, attentively.*)

KOTRLÝ: (*Without looking up*) What about her?

LORENCOVÁ: Why, she tried to cut her wrists . . .

(FOUSTKA *gets to his feet, agitated.*)

KOTRLÝ: (*Without looking up*) So it is true . . .

NEUWIRTH: (*Without turning round*) They say she's in the psycho ward . . .

LORENCOVÁ: The poor thing . . .

(FOUSTKA *sits down again. The* DEPUTY *enters, right, in ordinary clothes, holding hands with* PETRUŠKA, *who is wearing a white coat.* LORENCOVÁ *puts her mirror and compact in her coat pocket;* KOTRLÝ *folds his newspaper;* NEUWIRTH *puts back the book and turns round;* LORENCOVÁ, KOTRLÝ *and* FOUSTKA *get up.*)

KOTRLÝ: Good morning, sir.

DEPUTY: Good morning, friends. Sit down, sit down, please . . .

(LORENCOVÁ, KOTRLÝ *and* FOUSTKA *resume their seats. A short pause.*)

I don't see Vilma here.

FOUSTKA: She's had to go to the dentist.

(*A short pause.*)

DEPUTY: As you all know, we have a difficult task before us today. No one here – as the Director so aptly put it – has any intention of carrying out a witch-hunt. Truth must prevail, whoever suffers in the process. But all the more reason for us to remember that to seek the truth means to seek the *whole* and unembellished truth. The truth, my friends, is not just that which is shown to be true, but also that which it serves or for which it may be misused. As scientists we are only too acutely aware that by taking a fact

45

out of its context we can completely alter its meaning, indeed we can stand it on its head and thus turn truth into a lie and vice versa. In short, we must not lose sight of the living background of the actions we'll be judging and of the conclusions we come to. I hope I need not say any more – we're not little children, after all. Or are we?

KOTRLÝ: No, we're not.

DEPUTY: There you are, then! Who's feeding the pigeons today?

NEUWIRTH: I am...

DEPUTY: Splendid.

(*The* DIRECTOR *enters, right, in a white coat.* LORENCOVÁ, KOTRLÝ *and* FOUSTKA *rise quickly.*)

KOTRLÝ: Hi.

DIRECTOR: Hullo there, friends. Do sit down, please...

(LORENCOVÁ, KOTRLÝ *and* FOUSTKA *sit down. A short pause.*)

Where is Vilma?

DEPUTY: I asked the same question. I understand she's had to go to the dentist.

(*The* DIRECTOR *goes up to* KOTRLÝ *and holds out his hand to him.* KOTRLÝ *gets up.*)

DIRECTOR: (*To* KOTRLÝ) Did you sleep well?

KOTRLÝ: Yes, very well, thank you.

(*The* DIRECTOR *squeezes* KOTRLÝ's *elbow in a friendly fashion and turns to the others.* KOTRLÝ *sits down again.*)

DIRECTOR: As you all know, we have a difficult task before us today.

DEPUTY: That's just what I told our colleagues just now, Director.

DIRECTOR: We all know what is at stake, so you'll forgive me if I dispense with the preliminaries...

(VILMA *comes running in through the rear door. She seems out of breath, is carrying a large cardboard box.*)

VILMA: Sorry to be late, Director – I had an appointment with my dentist this morning, and just imagine...

DIRECTOR: Yes, I've heard. Sit down.

(VILMA *sits on the couch, puts the box down by her feet, and*

46

tries to communicate with FOUSTKA *in mime, then she indicates to him that she is keeping her fingers crossed.* LORENCOVÁ *leans over to her.*)

LORENCOVÁ: (*Softly*) What did you get?

VILMA: (*Softly*) Just my micro-oven back from the repair shop.

LORENCOVÁ: (*Softly*) Oh, I thought you'd bought a new hat.

VILMA: (*Softly.*) No . . .

DIRECTOR: Where was I?

KOTRLÝ: You were saying that we'll forgive you if you dispense with the preliminaries . . .

DIRECTOR: Oh yes. Let us dispense with the preliminaries and come straight to the point. Dr Foustka, would you please . . .

(*The* DIRECTOR *motions to* FOUSTKA *that he is to come forward;* FOUSTKA *gets up, crosses to centre stage and stands on the spot indicated by the* DIRECTOR.)

Good. Shall we begin?

FOUSTKA: By all means.

DIRECTOR: Well then, Dr Foustka, can you tell us whether it is true that for some time now . . .

(*The* SECRETARY *enters, right. He goes to the* DIRECTOR, *and whispers at length in his ear, the* DIRECTOR *nodding all the time and looking serious. The* SECRETARY *stops whispering, the* DIRECTOR *nods for the last time, the* SECRETARY *leaves, right.*)

Now, where was I?

KOTRLÝ: You were asking him if it is true that for some time . . .

DIRECTOR: Ah yes. Well then, Dr Foustka, can you tell us whether it is true that for some time now you have been engaged in the study of what is known as hermetic literature?

FOUSTKA: Yes, that's quite true.

DEPUTY: How long, would you say?

FOUSTKA: Oh, I can't say exactly . . .

DEPUTY: Approximately, then: six months, a year . . . ?

FOUSTKA: Something like that.

DIRECTOR: How many such books would you say you'd read in that time?

FOUSTKA: Oh, I don't know . . . I didn't count them.

DEPUTY: Approximately: Five? Thirty? Fifty?

FOUSTKA: Yes, maybe fifty . . .

DIRECTOR: Whom did you lend them to?

FOUSTKA: Lend them? Why, to no one.

DEPUTY: Come, come, Dr Foustka, are you trying to tell us that *nobody* borrowed these sought-after, rare and today practically unobtainable books? Your friends must have seen them, surely.

FOUSTKA: I don't invite friends to my place, and I don't lend books as a matter of principle.

DIRECTOR: All right. Now I must ask you to listen carefully, this is a most important question. I'm going to ask you. What made you take up this study in the first place? Why did you start taking such an interest in these things?

FOUSTKA: I had for some time been disturbed by the increasing interest taken by young people in everything that had to do with the so-called supernatural. This led finally to my deciding to write a study in which I would set out to show how diametrically opposed are the various idealistic and mystical beliefs of the past to our contemporary knowledge of the world. My project of course required . . .

DIRECTOR: (*Interrupts* FOUSTKA) That is exactly how we would have expected you to respond to my question. It does nothing, however, to explain the shocking fact that you yourself allegedly practised magic . . .

FOUSTKA: Well, hardly. I let it be known that I was practising it but did very little practising in actual fact . . .

DIRECTOR: But why would you do that?

FOUSTKA: It was the only way I could gain the confidence of someone as distrustful as are today's magicians.

DIRECTOR: I see. Are you saying you desired to be taken into their confidence? That is most interesting, most interesting. And to what extent, would you say, did you succeed?

FOUSTKA: To the modest extent, for the time being, of attracting the attention of a certain individual who has now visited me twice, as you have no doubt been informed . . .

DIRECTOR: Did that individual tell you *why* he visited you ?

48

FOUSTKA: He said he knew that I was interested in magical practices and that he was willing to initiate me in them.

DIRECTOR: And you accepted?

FOUSTKA: No, not in so many words – on the other hand I didn't explicitly turn him down. We are, so to speak, at the stage of preliminary soundings.

DEPUTY: What is he asking in return?

FOUSTKA: That I should, if need be, confirm that he has put himself at the disposal of science . . .

DEPUTY: Did you hear that, Director! Very clever, I must say . . .

DIRECTOR: I think the time has come to pose our crucial question: how do you explain that, on the one hand, you claim to have a scientific view of the world and therefore know that anyone pretending to be a magician is nothing but a charlatan, and yet, on the other, here you are trying to gain the confidence of magicians and when one of them actually seeks you out, you not only don't scorn him and throw him out, you actually intend to collaborate with him, indeed perhaps even shield him? Such obscure contacts and activities can hardly be brushed off by reference to critical scientific research.

FOUSTKA: This may seem naïve to you, but I simply felt, right from the outset, that I must not confine my efforts to help those who are being led astray by these charlatans – and my intention to do something effective about it – to mere theorizing and propaganda. I was and remain convinced that it would be dishonest of me if I were permanently to avoid tackling living reality just so as to keep a clear conscience and to try and deceive myself with illusions of the far-reaching effects of my theoretical struggle. I simply felt that having taken the first step, it was up to me to continue the journey, and that it was my duty as a citizen to place my theoretical knowledge at the disposal of the campaign to unmask and bring to book the perpetrators of these activities. Now at the Institute we are all the time professing to be fighting against pseudo-science, mysticism and superstition – and yet we would be hard put to it to

point a finger at even one of those who spread these poisons. And not just us – it is nothing short of amazing how little is known about these matters, how unsuccessful all the attempts to infiltrate these murky waters. No wonder then that the disease is spreading so rapidly. That is why I decided to gain the confidence of these people, penetrate their circle and collect damning evidence at the very source. I can hardly do this without pretending to share at least some of their beliefs in spirits, initiations, evocations, magic happenings, incubi and succubi, and all the rest of that nonsense. I may even have to take an oath of silence if I wish to string them along. In short, I've decided to be an inconspicuous, lone soldier in this – how shall I put it? – in this secret war, having come to the conclusion that my expertise makes me particularly suitable for this task . . .
(*A long pause. All his listeners are taken aback, looking at one another in puzzlement, then they all fix their eyes on the* DIRECTOR.)

DIRECTOR: You mean to say that you . . . that . . . well, I . . .
(*A pause.*)
Well, I cannot deny that it would be a feather in our cap if the Institute could bring off some such successful coup. Dr Foustka is doubtless right when he says that no propaganda brochures ever won a war . . .

DEPUTY: (*To* FOUSTKA) Am I to understand then that you would be willing to provide us with a record of any and every meeting you might have, either with this individual of yours or with anyone else?

FOUSTKA: But of course – that's why I've got into this in the first place . . .

DEPUTY: Well, I cannot deny that that would be a feather in our cap, as the Director has already pointed out. Tell me one thing, though – why is it that this . . . this commendable initiative of yours has only come to our notice now, when certain – it would seem unsubstantiated – accusations have been levelled against you? Why did you not inform us about your intentions and about the first steps you took right from the beginning?

FOUSTKA: Yes, I can see now that that was a mistake. I approached the whole business as a scientist about to undertake a new line of research. As you know, we scientists tend to work on our own, we are not in the habit of reporting every step, and I thought it would be time enough to report progress when I had actually achieved something worthy of reporting. It just did not occur to me that a tit-bit of information from some uninformed source could possibly shake the confidence I had hitherto enjoyed at the Institute.

DIRECTOR: That is hardly surprising, wouldn't you say? However noble your idea, what you have done is so out of the ordinary and, if I may say so, so unexpected in your particular case that we cannot be blamed if at first we misunderstood your motives.

DEPUTY: That is hardly surprising, wouldn't you say?

DIRECTOR: But never mind – let us not waste any more time, we all have work to do. You have convinced me that it *was* just a misunderstanding, and all that remains to be said is that I am glad that it has now been satisfactorily cleared up. Needless to say, I appreciate what you are trying to do and I shall see to it that your remarkable initiative is suitably rewarded – particularly once you get into the habit of keeping a record of your researches and regularly passing it on to us. Any questions, anyone?

(*An embarrassed pause.*)

Nothing? In that case, let me spring my little surprise: tomorrow's social in the Institute garden will be in fancy dress!

LORENCOVÁ: Fabulous!

KOTRLÝ: What a marvellous idea!

DEPUTY: Isn't it? I quite agree . . .

LORENCOVÁ: What theme will it have?

DIRECTOR: Obviously – Witches' Sabbath!

(*An excited murmur.*)

A congregation of devils, witches, magicians and sorcerers. We'll do it in style. Originally I had thought of it simply as an attempt to enliven our tradition of Institute socials by the addition of a parodic element. It seemed to me that if, in the evening, we were to laugh at that which, during the day, we have to combat with a cool head and straight face, we could enhance our own attitude to our work – in keeping with the latest findings of costume therapy. By momentarily ridiculing the problem, we would be emphasizing its lasting gravity; by making light of it, drawing attention to its weightiness; by standing aside from it, drawing closer to it. Now, however, I see that, thanks to the coincidence of Dr Foustka's revelations, there is also another way of looking at it: as a light-hearted tribute to his admirable efforts, which may well necessitate not only disguise in the figurative sense of the world, but also disguise in the literal sense, if he, for instance, has to infiltrate a black mass.

(*Polite laughter.*)

But never mind – let us not waste any more time, we all have work to do. Perhaps we can consider this to be a bit of light relief after our serious session, which has been so satisfactorily concluded. Whose turn is it to feed the pigeons?

NEUWIRTH: Mine . . .

DIRECTOR: Splendid. (*To* KOTRLÝ) Now, don't forget, Vilém!
(*Curtain falls.*)

SCENE EIGHT

VILMA's *flat. As the curtain rises,* FOUSTKA *is sitting in his underpants on the edge of the bed,* VILMA, *wearing a lace negligée, is combing her hair by the dressing-table – the same situation as at the beginning of Scene Four.*

FOUSTKA: Once you let him in I'm sure he'd expect a little more than a kiss on the cheek! At the very least he'd want to dance with you.

VILMA: Henry, please leave it alone. After all, I don't give *you* the third degree – even though I have more reason than you.

52

(*A short pause, then* FOUSTKA *gets up and starts pacing up and down the room, lost in thought.* VILMA *stops combing her hair and follows him with her eyes.*)

What is it?

FOUSTKA: What's what?

VILMA: You started off so nicely ...

FOUSTKA: Somehow I don't feel like it today ...

VILMA: Does it excite you too much?

FOUSTKA: No, it's not that.

VILMA: So what's wrong?

FOUSTKA: As if you didn't know ...

VILMA: But I don't!

FOUSTKA: You don't, do you? Who shopped me, who told the Director that the magician had come to see me?

(VILMA *freezes, then throws her comb down, jumps up and looks at* FOUSTKA, *horrified.*)

VILMA: For heaven's sake, Henry, you don't really think ...

FOUSTKA: No one else at the Institute knew about it.

VILMA: Are you crazy? Why should I do a thing like that? Quite apart from insulting me by believing for a moment that I would be capable of denouncing anybody to that idiot, how can you think that I would inform on *you*? I would as soon go and inform on myself! Don't you know how much I want you to be happy and how much I worry about you? What possible reason would I suddenly have to try and destroy you? And with you, to destroy myself – our relationship – our life together – our make-believe jealousy – our love, which you have recently confirmed so deliciously by exhibiting *real* jealousy – our memories of all the sunny moments of pure happiness we have known together ... Why, it would be sheer madness!

FOUSTKA: It may well be the memory of those sunny moments that provided the motive force for your action. What do I know about women? Perhaps you wanted to take revenge on me because of Maggie – or perhaps you were scared of that invalid and thought that in this way you could extricate me from what you considered to be his clutches ...

(VILMA *runs to the bed, throws herself face down on the*

53

pillow, and starts crying. FOUSTKA *stands there helplessly,*
looking at VILMA, *then he sits down gingerly on the bed and*
strokes her hair.)
Come on now, Vilma...
(*A pause.* VILMA *goes on sobbing.*)
I didn't mean it...
(*A pause.* VILMA *goes on sobbing.*)
It was just a joke...
(*A pause.* VILMA *goes on sobbing.*)
I thought I'd add a new twist to our game...
(*A pause.* VILMA *sits up abruptly, wiping her eyes with her*
handkerchief and sniffling. When she has recovered her
composure, she says coolly:)
VILMA: Go away!
(FOUSTKA *attempts to stroke her, but* VILMA *pushes him away*
and shouts.)
Don't touch me! Go away!
FOUSTKA: Really, Vilma. Why're you making such a fuss?
You've often asked me to say far worse things to you...
VILMA: That was different. Do you realize what you've done?
You've accused me in so many words of spying on you!
Kindly get dressed and go away – and don't ever try to
patch up what you've just so brutally destroyed.
FOUSTKA: Are you serious?
VILMA: Let's end it here and now. It would have come to that
sooner or later...
FOUSTKA: You mean on account of that dancer?
VILMA: No, not that...
FOUSTKA: Why then?
VILMA: I've lost my respect for you.
FOUSTKA: Well, that's a new one on me.
VILMA: It's only just happened, that's why. Today, if you must
know, at the Institute – it struck me then, when I saw how
shamelessly you got yourself out of a hole. In front of
everybody, to tell the Director that you'd act as a stool-
pigeon for him. And now, to cap it all, you come and
accuse *me* of acting like one! Can't you see how absurd it all
is? What's got into you? Is this really you I'm talking to?

54

Or has some devil truly possessed you? That wretched fellow has addled your brain, I expect. God knows what he's done to you, what kind of magic he's trying out on you . . .

(FOUSTKA *gets up and starts pacing up and down the room.*)

FOUSTKA: All right, I'll tell you what he has done. No magic tricks: he is merely helping me to know myself better and to counter the bad things lying dormant inside me. Listen, my acting as a stool-pigeon, as you put it, not only served to save me but also to help him – the only way I could. If they know that I'm in control, they'll leave him alone. Anyway, how could I keep my suspicion that you betrayed me to myself? What kind of a relationship would that be? You may have said it inadvertently, perhaps to someone you trusted, or perhaps it was overheard by someone whose presence you were unaware of.

VILMA: I didn't say anything to anybody, inadvertently or otherwise – and it's not your expressing your suspicion that I object to – even though you did it so brutally and are now, belatedly, trying to wriggle out of it – what I mind is that you could even *think* such a thing. If you can do that, even for a minute, then I don't see how we can stay together.

(*A pause.* FOUSTKA *sinks into the armchair and gazes dispiritedly in front of him.*)

FOUSTKA: What an idiot I was to say anything. But then, I always manage to mess things up, don't I? What am I going to do without you? How can I go on living if I'm to lose you?

VILMA: Now you're going to feel sorry for yourself, are you?

FOUSTKA: Do you remember what we said to each other that day by the river under the elms?

VILMA: It'll do you no good to remind me. You've hurt me too much for you to talk your way out of it by dredging up our memories. And anyway, I asked you to go . . .

FOUSTKA: I know what it is – you're expecting the dancer, aren't you?

VILMA: I'm not expecting anybody – I just want to be alone.

(*A short pause.* FOUSTKA *suddenly jumps up, runs across to* VILMA, *pushes her down on the bed and roughly seizes her by the throat.*)

FOUSTKA: (*In a menacing voice*) You're lying, you bitch!

VILMA: (*Cries out*) Help!

(FOUSTKA *is throttling* VILMA. *The door bell rings.* FOUSTKA *lets go of* VILMA, *jumps away from the bed, remains standing there for a few moments, then slowly goes to the armchair and sits down heavily.* VILMA *gets up, hurriedly arranges her hair and her clothing, and goes to the door. She opens it to find the* DANCER *outside, a bunch of violets held behind his back.*)

DANCER: Sorry to show up so late. I only wanted to give you . . .

(*The* DANCER *hands the flowers to* VILMA.)

VILMA: Thanks. Do come in, won't you.

(*The* DANCER, *surprised, looks first at* VILMA, *then at* FOUSTKA, *who is sitting slumped in the armchair, staring vacantly in front of him.*)

He's not well . . . I'd be glad if you could stay. I'm afraid that . . .

DANCER: Is it his heart?

VILMA: Probably.

DANCER: Why don't we dance a little? Maybe it will cheer him up . . .

(*Curtain falls.*)

SCENE NINE

FOUSTKA's *flat.* FOUSTKA *is alone, in a dressing-gown, pacing up and down the room. There is a knock on the door.* FOUSTKA *stops pacing, hesitates for a moment, then calls out.*

FOUSTKA: (*Calls out*) Who is it?

HOUBOVÁ: (*Off stage*) It's only me, Doctor.

FOUSTKA: (*Calling*) Come in, Mrs Houbová.

(HOUBOVÁ *enters.*)

HOUBOVÁ: You have a visitor . . .

FOUSTKA: Have I? Who is it?

HOUBOVÁ: It's him again. You know, the one who . . .

FOUSTKA: I know – smells.

HOUBOVÁ: That's him.

FOUSTKA: Tell him to come in.

(*A short pause.* HOUBOVÁ *stands still, embarrassed.*)

Well, what is it?

HOUBOVÁ: I don't know how . . .

FOUSTKA: What is the matter?

HOUBOVÁ: Look 'ere, Doctor, I'm just an ignorant woman . . .
I know it's not my place to give you advice . . .

FOUSTKA: No, go on, what is it you want to tell me?

HOUBOVÁ: I know it's none of my business, but if I were you, I
wouldn't trust him. I can't explain . . . and I don't know
why he comes here in the first place, but he . . . well, he
gives me the creeps . . .

FOUSTKA: You let him in readily enough last time.

HOUBOVÁ: 'Cause I was afraid of him, that's why.

FOUSTKA: Well, I know he looks somewhat odd, but he is quite
harmless, you know. Or, more precisely, he's too
insignificant to be in a position to do too much damage.

HOUBOVÁ: I don't know why you have any truck with such as
'im. A gentleman like you.

FOUSTKA: Oh, come, Mrs Houbová, I'm over eighteen and
perfectly capable of looking after myself.

HOUBOVÁ: I'm afraid for your sake. And is it surprising – why,
I remember you as a little three-year-old, me not having
children of my own . . .

FOUSTKA: Yes, yes, I know. Thank you for your concern – you
must not think I don't appreciate it, but in this case you
really need have no fear. Just let him in and stop worrying.

(HOUBOVÁ *leaves the room, leaving the door ajar.*)

HOUBOVÁ: (*Off stage*) You're to go in . . .

(FISTULA *enters, holding his paper bag in his hand.*
HOUBOVÁ *stands in the doorway, following him with her eyes,
then she shakes her head and closes the door.* FISTULA *grins
vacuously and makes straight for the couch, sits down, takes his
shoes off, removes his slippers from the bag and puts them on,*

replacing them in the bag with his shoes, then lays the bag on the floor at his feet. He looks up at FOUSTKA *and grins.*)

FISTULA: Well . . . ?

FOUSTKA: Well, what?

FISTULA: I'm waiting for you to start your usual litany . . .

FOUSTKA: What're you talking about?

FISTULA: Telling me to get out and so on . . .

(FOUSTKA *paces up and down the room, then sits down at his desk.*)

FOUSTKA: I see. Now look, I'd just like to say a couple of things. Firstly, I've realized that there's no way I can be rid of you, so it's a waste of time and effort to try. Secondly, without in any way overestimating your so-called stimulating influence, I have come to the conclusion that the time spent with you does not have to be entirely wasted. If I have to serve you for your purposes, there is no reason why you should not reciprocate by serving mine in return. Did you not at the outset offer to initiate me into your mysteries if I agree to shield you? Well, I accept your offer.

FISTULA: Yes, I knew you would in the end, which explains why I was so persistent. How nice to see my persistence rewarded at last. But let me not overdo the modesty – I don't ascribe your decision to my persistence alone, but also to the undoubted success of our collaboration . . .

FOUSTKA: What success do you have in mind?

FISTULA: Well, not only have you managed to keep your job at the Institute, you have actually strengthened your position there. I was delighted to notice that you in this case even managed to avoid Smíchovský's Compensation Syndrome – now that is what I call progress . . .

FOUSTKA: If by that you mean that I've jettisoned all my moral principles and left myself open to whatever you may choose to waken in me, then you are very much mistaken. I have not changed, I have only gained a little more self-control, which enables me to know exactly how far I can go without the risk of doing anything I'd later have reason to regret. (FISTULA *grows somewhat agitated, looks around the room.*) What's the matter with you?

FISTULA: It's nothing . . .

FOUSTKA: You look scared. I've never seen that before.
Surprising that it should happen now, just when I have
promised to shield you.

(FISTULA *takes off his slippers and sighing, rubs the soles of his
feet with both hands.*)

Are you in pain?

FISTULA: It's nothing . . . it'll pass . . .

(*After a while* FISTULA *puts his slippers on again. Suddenly he
bursts out laughing.*)

FOUSTKA: What's so funny?

FISTULA: May I be absolutely frank?

FOUSTKA: Be my guest.

FISTULA: You are!

FOUSTKA: You're laughing at me, is that it? Of all the bloody
cheek!

(FISTULA *grows serious and looks at the floor. After a few
moments he glances sharply at* FOUSTKA.)

FISTULA: Look here, Doctor. There's nothing wrong with you
saving your skin by dint of a little skulduggery – after all,
that's precisely the procedure that Haajah and I . . .

FOUSTKA: Who?

FISTULA: Haajah, the spirit of politics. We prompted you to act
as you did. But you shouldn't have forgotten the rules of
the game.

FOUSTKA: Rules? What game? What the devil are you talking
about?

FISTULA: Does it not occur to you that, like everything else,
our collaboration also has its rules? Do away with your
scruples as much as you like – you know that I'm all in
favour of that. But you really shouldn't try and cheat the
one who is guiding you on this exciting, I might perhaps
say revolutionary, path you know. Revolution, too, has its
rules. Last time you called me a devil. Just imagine for a
moment that I really am one. How do you think I'd react to
your amateurish attempt to fool me?

FOUSTKA: Fool you? But I wasn't . . .

FISTULA: Look, even if we didn't explicitly promise, surely it

59

should have been obvious that we would not mention our collaboration to anyone, much less write official reports for those in authority who take a negative view of it. I don't think I exaggerate when I say that we had begun – however tentatively – to trust each other. If you failed to grasp that we had this unwritten gentleman's agreement and chose to flout it, then that was your first serious error. You have read enough books on the subject to know that even in my sphere there are limits that cannot be ignored. Surely you must realize that, being able to play with the entire world, we have to put our trust in contacts that simply cannot be trifled with. To lie to a liar is fine, to lie to those who speak the truth is permissible, but to lie to the very powers which furnish us with the ability to lie and ensure that we do so with impunity – that's really unforgivable. As for him (*He points up at the ceiling*), he loads man with a multitude of unrealistic commandments, and so he has no alternative but to forgive, from time to time. Others, on the contrary, liberate man from all these impossible commands, and as a result of course they do not have the need, the opportunity, or ultimately the ability to forgive. Even if they had, they could scarcely forgive someone who goes back on the agreement that opens up all this boundless freedom. Their entire world would collapse, were they to do that. The truth of the matter is, that only by undertaking to be faithful to the authority that gives us this freedom can we hope to be freed. Do you follow my drift?

(FOUSTKA *who, while* FISTULA *was speaking, exhibited increasing signs of nervousness, gets up and starts pacing up and down the room. A long pause.* FISTULA *does not take his eyes off* FOUSTKA, *who suddenly stops behind his desk, leans against it as if it were a lectern, and turns to* FISTULA.)

FOUSTKA: Yes, I understand exactly what you're saying, but I'm afraid you fail to understand *me*.

FISTULA: You don't say.

FOUSTKA: The understanding you are obviously referring to could only be considered as an attempt at treachery on my part by someone who was unaware of the reason why I was able to give it in the first place.

FISTULA: You did it to save your skin . . .

FOUSTKA: Yes, of course, but what would that have been worth had it been paid for by treachery? Do you take me for an idiot? I could give that undertaking only because I had made up my mind from the start not only not to keep it, but at the same time to make the best use of the position I have gained with its help – naturally in close consultation with you, in the spirit of our agreement and for our benefit. In other words, I am now in a position to know exactly what the other side is up to and to flood them with our disinformation; I can cover our tracks and provide them with false ones; and I can use all this to help those of us who are in danger and sink those who endanger us. Don't you see, I can serve our cause like an agent planted in the very midst of the enemy, indeed, at the head of the very department whose job it is to wage war against us. I am surprised and disappointed that you have failed to grasp and appreciate my intentions.

(FOUSTKA *sits down.* FISTULA *jumps to his feet, starts to chortle and hop around the room. Suddenly he stops and, serious again, turns to* FOUSTKA.)

FISTULA: Even though you may well have invented this explanation on the spur of the moment – so be it, I accept it. To give you your last chance, you understand. We, too, can occasionally forgive and offer the culprit the opportunity to reform. If a little while ago I told you otherwise, then that was only to scare you and coax you to make this quite unambiguous offer, thus saving you from the very edge of the precipice. As you can see, I really am not the devil – luckily for you: the piece of treachery you have been able to get away with in my case would have cost you dear if I were.

(FOUSTKA *is obviously relieved; on a sudden impulse he comes up to* FISTULA *and embraces him.* FISTULA *jumps away from him, begins to rub his arms, his teeth chattering.*)

Man, your temperature must be a hundred below!

FOUSTKA: (*Laughs*) Not quite . . .
  (*Curtain falls.*)

SCENE TEN

We are again in the Institute garden. Everything is the same as in Scene Three, except that the bench is now right and the refreshments table left. When the curtain rises, the music grows softer and changes its character, just as in Scene Three; it again – unless stated otherwise – forms a background to the action. On stage are the two LOVERS *and* FOUSTKA. *The* LOVERS *can be seen dancing at the back, as they will continue to do throughout – the summer-house is thus empty.* FOUSTKA *is sitting on the bench, lost in thought. All three are dressed in accordance with the 'magical theme' of the evening:* FOUSTKA *has come as Faust. Where the text does not provide a more exact description of the costumes or masks, it is to be understood that all the characters appearing in this scene are dressed and made up in the same spirit, and it is left to the producers how this is done. It is to be expected that the costumes and masks will include some of the traditional ones used in the theatre for this type of scene – for instance, the colours black and red will predominate, the characters will be wearing various pendants and amulets, ladies will have frizzy wigs, and there will be a profusion of devils' tails, hooves and chains. The actors, however, behave as if there were no such costumes, their demeanour being just the same as in Scene Three. A long pause. Then* LORENCOVÁ *appears on the right, carrying a broom under her arm. She crosses the stage towards the refreshments table and pours herself a drink. A pause.*
FOUSTKA: Do you know if the Director is here yet?
LORENCOVÁ: No, I don't.
  (*A pause.* LORENCOVÁ *finishes her drink, puts down the glass, and goes off, left. A little later we see her dancing, alone with her broom, at the back. A pause. The* DEPUTY *enters, left.*)
DEPUTY: Have you seen Petruška?
FOUSTKA: She's not been here . . .
  (*The* DEPUTY *shakes his head, as if in disbelief, and goes off, right. A little later we see him, moving around on the dance-*

floor on his own. FOUSTKA *gets up, crosses to the table, and pours himself a drink. The* DIRECTOR *and* KOTRLÝ *come in from the right, holding hands. Unless stated otherwise, they will remain like that throughout. The* DIRECTOR, *strikingly dressed as a devil, is wearing a pair of horns. The* DIRECTOR *and* KOTRLÝ *pay no attention to* FOUSTKA; *they come to a halt centre stage.* FOUSTKA *watches them.*)

DIRECTOR: (*To* KOTRLÝ) Where are you thinking of putting it?

KOTRLÝ: Seems to me the summer-house would be the best place . . .

DIRECTOR: Yes, I think you're right. For safety reasons, if nothing else . . .

KOTRLÝ: I'll light it in the gardener's shed and then carry it over. It takes a few minutes to get going. I'll put it in the summer-house and a minute or two later – whoosh!

(*The* DIRECTOR *and* KOTRLÝ *start off to the left.*)

FOUSTKA: Oh, Director . . .

(*The* DIRECTOR *and* KOTRLÝ *stop.*)

DIRECTOR: Yes, what is it, Doctor Foustka?

FOUSTKA: Have you got a minute?

DIRECTOR: Sorry, my friend, but not just now . . .

(*The* DIRECTOR *and* KOTRLÝ *go off, left. A little later we see them dancing together at the back. Glass in hand,* FOUSTKA *returns to the bench, lost in thought, and sits down. The music grows noticeably louder, it's a well-known tango.* VILMA *and the* DANCER *come running in, left, and dance together, the* DANCER – *obviously a true professional* – *leading her in some complicated tango movements.* FOUSTKA *sits there, motionless, looking at them. The music reaches a crescendo,* VILMA *and the* DANCER *end their dance with a final flourish. The music grows softer and changes its character again.* VILMA *and the* DANCER *are out of breath but obviously very happy; they hold hands and smile at each other.*)

FOUSTKA: Having a good time?

VILMA: As you can see . . .

(*The* DEPUTY *having left the dance-floor, enters, left.*)

DEPUTY: Have you seen Petruška?

VILMA: She's not been here . . .

(*The* DEPUTY *shakes his head, as if in disbelief, and goes off, right. A little later we see him, moving around the dance-floor on his own.* VILMA *seizes the* DANCER *by the hand and leads him off, right. A little later we again see them dancing at the back.* FOUSTKA *gets up, crosses to the refreshments table, and pours himself a drink. The* DIRECTOR *and* KOTRLÝ *come in from the right, having left the dance-floor; they are holding hands. They pay no attention to* FOUSTKA *and come to a halt centre stage.* FOUSTKA *watches them.*)

KOTRLÝ: (*To the* DIRECTOR) How do I know the right moment has come?

DIRECTOR: Oh, just pick your own time. Or I'll give you a sign ... I have other things on my mind right now ...

KOTRLÝ: What is it?

DIRECTOR: Can you guarantee that nothing will go wrong?

KOTRLÝ: What could go wrong?

DIRECTOR: Well, can't something catch fire, or someone might suffocate ...

KOTRLÝ: No, don't worry.

(*The* DIRECTOR *and* KOTRLÝ *start off to the left.*)

FOUSTKA: Oh, Director ...

(*The* DIRECTOR *and* KOTRLÝ *stop.*)

DIRECTOR: Yes, what is it, Doctor Foustka?

FOUSTKA: I'm sorry, I know you have a lot of other things on your mind, but this won't take a minute, and ...

DIRECTOR: No, really, not just now ...

(*The* SECRETARY *enters, right. He goes to the* DIRECTOR *and whispers at length in his ear, the* DIRECTOR *nodding all the time. While this is going on,* LORENCOVÁ *enters, right, having left the dance-floor. She is still carrying her broom and remains standing, right, by the bench, looking at the* SECRETARY. *After a while the* SECRETARY *stops whispering in the* DIRECTOR'S *ear, the* DIRECTOR *nods for the last time, then goes off, left, with* KOTRLÝ. *A little later we see them dancing together at the back. The* SECRETARY *crosses to the right, in* LORENCOVÁ'S *direction.* LORENCOVÁ *is smiling at him, the* SECRETARY *stops right in front of her and they gaze into each other's eyes, then the* SECRETARY, *without taking his eyes off*

64

her, takes away her broom, carefully lays it on the ground, and embraces her. She returns his embrace, they stand there gazing tenderly at each other, then they kiss. A few moments later they go off, their arms around each other's waist. A little later we see them dancing together at the back. FOUSTKA *goes back to the bench, glass in hand, and sits down, lost in thought. Suddenly he sits up, as if listening: off stage we hear a girl's voice singing, to the accompaniment of the background music, Ophelia's song from* Hamlet.)

MAGGIE: (*Sings off stage*) And will he not come again?
And will he not come again?
No, no, he is dead:
Go to thy death-bed:
He never will come again.
(MAGGIE *appears, left. She is barefoot, has let her hair down and is wearing a wreath of wild flowers, a white nightgown which is stamped at the bottom with a large rubber stamp:* PSYCHIATRY. *She approaches slowly, singing. As she comes towards* FOUSTKA, *he gets up, startled.*)
(*Sings*) He never will come again.
His beard was as white as snow,
All flaxen was his poll:
He is gone, he is gone,
And we cast away moan:
God ha' mercy on his soul!
God ha' mercy on his soul!

FOUSTKA: (*Calls out*) Maggie!

MAGGIE: Where is the handsome Prince of Denmark?
(FOUSTKA *retreats in horror, followed by* MAGGIE; *they slowly circle the stage.*)

FOUSTKA: What for God's sake are you doing here? Have you run away?

MAGGIE: Please tell him, if you see him, that it cannot all be happening of its own accord, there has to be a more profound will at work, willing our existence, the world, all nature . . .

FOUSTKA: Maggie, don't you recognize me? It's me, Henry . . .

MAGGIE: Or does it not strike you as if the cosmos had actually

65

determined to see itself one day through our eyes and to put the questions which we are now putting, with our lips?

FOUSTKA: Go back, Maggie, they will help you get better . . . everything will be all right again . . . you'll see . . .

MAGGIE: (*Sings*) How should I your true love know
    From another one?
By his cockle hat and staff,
    And his sandal shoon.

(MAGGIE *goes off, right, her song can still be heard growing fainter, though we can no longer distinguish the words.*
FOUSTKA *agitated, crosses to the table and quickly pours himself a drink, downs it in a single gulp and pours another. The* DIRECTOR *and* KOTRLÝ *come in, right, having left the dance-floor. They are holding hands and pay no attention to* FOUSTKA.)

DIRECTOR: (*To* KOTRLÝ) At the very least, I'm sure he wanted to dance with you . . .

KOTRLÝ: Please leave it alone! Can't you find something more interesting to talk about?

DIRECTOR: Did he or didn't he?

KOTRLÝ: All right, if you must know, he did. And that's all I'm going to say . . .

(*The* DIRECTOR *and* KOTRLÝ *have slowly crossed the stage and are about to go off, left.*)

FOUSTKA: Oh, Director . . .

(*The* DIRECTOR *and* KOTRLÝ *stop.*)

DIRECTOR: Yes, what is it, Doctor Foustka?

(*At that moment we hear a cry of pain from the bushes behind the bench.*)

NEUWIRTH: (*Off stage*) Ouch!

(*The* DIRECTOR, KOTRLÝ *and* FOUSTKA *look, surprised, at the bench.* NEUWIRTH *comes out of the bushes, holding his evidently injured ear, and moaning.*)

KOTRLÝ: What's happened, Alois?

NEUWIRTH: It's nothing . . .

DIRECTOR: What's wrong with your ear? Have you hurt it?

(NEUWIRTH *nods.*)

KOTRLÝ: Did something bite you?

(NEUWIRTH *nods, motioning with his head in the direction of the bushes from which he had come and out of which he is now followed by an embarrassed* PETRUŠKA. *She is nervously rearranging her costume and hair. The* DIRECTOR *and* KOTRLÝ *exchange significant glances and smile.* NEUWIRTH, *holding his ear and moaning, shuffles off to the right and disappears.* PETRUŠKA *shyly flits across the stage to the refreshments table and, her hand shaking a little, pours herself a drink, which she hurriedly drinks. The* DIRECTOR *and* KOTRLÝ *are about to leave.*)

FOUSTKA: Oh, Director . . .

(*The* DIRECTOR *and* KOTRLÝ *stop.*)

DIRECTOR: Yes, what is it, Doctor Foustka?

(*The* DEPUTY *enters, left. He does not at first see* PETRUŠKA, *who is hidden behind* FOUSTKA.)

DEPUTY: Have you seen Petruška?

(PETRUŠKA *comes up to the* DEPUTY, *smiles at him and takes his hand; from now on they will hold hands as before.*)

Where have you been, sweetheart?

(PETRUŠKA *whispers in the* DEPUTY's *ear. He listens attentively, then nods contentedly. The* DIRECTOR *and* KOTRLÝ *are about to leave.*)

FOUSTKA: Oh, Director . . .

(*The* DIRECTOR *and* KOTRLÝ *stop.*)

DIRECTOR: Yes, what is it, Doctor Foustka?

FOUSTKA: I'm sorry, I know you have a lot of other things on your mind, but on the other hand . . . I really must . . . having learned my lesson, I want to make sure nothing is neglected . . . I have made certain discoveries, which I have written down in my report . . .

(FOUSTKA *searches his pockets, looking for a piece of paper. The* DIRECTOR *and the* DEPUTY *exchange significant glances and come forward, still holding* KOTRLÝ *and* PETRUŠKA *by the hand. All four form a semi-circle centre stage around* FOUSTKA. *A short pause.*)

DIRECTOR: Don't bother . . .

(FOUSTKA *looks up, surprised, first at the* DIRECTOR, *then at the others. A tense pause.*)

FOUSTKA: But I thought . . .

(*Another tense pause, broken by the* DIRECTOR.)

DIRECTOR: (*In severe tones*) I'm not interested in what you thought, I'm not interested in your piece of paper, I'm not interested in you. You see, my dear sir, the comedy is over.

FOUSTKA: I don't understand . . . what comedy?

DIRECTOR: I'm afraid you have been too clever by half, and you have badly underestimated us, taking us for much greater idiots than we really are . . .

DEPUTY: You still don't understand?

FOUSTKA: No, I don't.

DIRECTOR: All right, then, I'll give it to you straight. We of course knew all along what you thought of us, we knew that you were merely pretending to be loyal while concealing your true views and interests. Nevertheless, we decided to give you one last chance and so we pretended to believe your fairy-tale about working for us undercover, so to speak. We were curious to see how you would conduct yourself after the scare we gave you, whether perhaps you might at last see the error of your ways and come to your senses. And what did you do? You chose to spit at our helping hand, and by so doing you have sealed your fate.

FOUSTKA: That's not true!

DIRECTOR: You know only too well that it is.

FOUSTKA: I suppose you can prove it?

DIRECTOR: (*To the* DEPUTY) Shall we oblige?

DEPUTY: I'd say yes. Let's.

(*The* DIRECTOR *puts two fingers in his mouth and gives a piercing whistle.* FISTULA, *who has all this time been hidden in the summer-house, jumps out of his hiding place.* FOUSTKA *sees him and grows agitated.* FISTULA *quickly limps towards the* DIRECTOR.)

FISTULA: Yes, boss, what can I do for you?

DIRECTOR: What did Foustka tell you yesterday?

FISTULA: He said he would pretend to be working undercover for you, while in fact, in cahoots with those you're fighting against, sabotaging your intelligence service at every step. He said, and I quote, that he would be our – that is, *their* –

agent in the very midst of the enemy . . .

FOUSTKA: (*Shouts*) He's lying!

DIRECTOR: What did you say? Can you repeat that?

FOUSTKA: I said he was lying.

DIRECTOR: How dare you? How dare you insinuate that one of my finest external collaborators and a personal friend of long standing is a liar. Fistula *never* lies to us!

DEPUTY: Just what I was about to say, Director, Fistula *never* lies to us!

(LORENCOVÁ *and the* SECRETARY *enter, left, at the same time as the* LOVERS, *all four having left the dance-floor; both couples are holding hands. They join the others, inconspicuously enlarging the semi-circle around* FOUSTKA.)

FOUSTKA: (*To* FISTULA) So I fell into your trap, after all, didn't I?

FISTULA: I'm sorry, Doctor . . . (*To the* DIRECTOR) He still has his title, does he?

DIRECTOR: Oh, fuck all that . . .

FISTULA: Well, I'm sorry, Henry, but here you go again – simplifying everything. Did I not let you know all along that you had a range of choices and that you alone could decide your fate? You did not fall into any trap of mine, you came a cropper thanks to your own pride, which led you to believe that you could play both ends against the middle and get away with it. Have you forgotten the pains I took to explain to you that man has to respect *someone* in authority – whoever that someone may be – unless he wants to come to a bad end? And that even revolution has its rules? Did I say that or didn't I? I really cannot see how I could have made things any clearer to you. So my conscience is clear . . . I did what I could. I'm afraid it's your funeral if you failed to understand . . .

DIRECTOR: As always, Fistula is absolutely right. You simply cannot serve all masters, and at the same time deceive them all. You can't just take and give nothing in return. Every one of us has to decide where he stands.

DEPUTY: Just what I was about to say, Director. Every one of us has to decide where he stands.

(The music grows noticeably louder – we again hear the tango as before. VILMA *and the* DANCER *come running in, having left the dance-floor. They run through the semi-circle around* FOUSTKA *to centre stage, where they again execute some complicated tango steps, the* DANCER *bending* VILMA *right over so that the top of her head almost brushes the ground. The music again grows softer, and* VILMA *and the* DANCER, *holding hands like all the other couples, join the semi-circle.)*

FOUSTKA: Isn't it paradoxical that now when I have finally lost and my knowledge can serve no purpose, I'm beginning to understand it all. Fistula is right: I am a conceited idiot who thought he could use the devil without having to sign his soul away to him. As if the devil could be deceived.

FISTULA: Hold on a minute! Just hold on there. I never said that there is such a thing as the devil!

FOUSTKA: That's as maybe – but I'm saying it. And he's right here among us!

FISTULA: I see – you mean me, of course?

FOUSTKA: Hardly. You're just a subordinate little demon.

DIRECTOR: I know the way your mind works, Foustka, and I see that, through me, you would like to point an accusing finger at modern science and denounce it as the true source of all evil. Am I right?

FOUSTKA: No, you're not. Through you I merely wish to denounce the arrogance of intolerant, self-regarding power, which uses science as a handy bow with which to shoot down anything that threatens it. That is to say, anything which does not owe its authority to that power, or stems from some authority outside.

DIRECTOR: Is that the legacy you wish to leave the world, Foustka?

FOUSTKA: Yes!

DIRECTOR: Somewhat banal, wouldn't you say? In countries where they don't believe in censorship, any sports reporter worth his salt scatters such pearls of wisdom by the wayside. However, a legacy is a legacy, so let me demonstrate how tolerant I am – despite what others may think of me – by overlooking my objections and applauding you.

70

(*The* DIRECTOR *starts to clap, the others join in, one by one. At the same time the music grows more insistent – a piece of hard rock, wild and throbbing. If possible, the music should be composed so ingeniously that this would be a variation on the themes played before the performance and during the intervals, so that there is a connection between the stormy finale and the earlier music. The clapping soon turns rhythmical, in time to the music, which grows in volume until it is almost deafening. All those present, except* FOUSTKA, *gradually succumb to the rhythm – first they just move slightly in tune with the music, then they sway from side to side, until they are all dancing – at first each on his or her own, then in pairs, finally all together. The dance grows wilder all the time, until it turns into an orgiastic carnival.* FOUSTKA *takes no part in the dance, merely stumbling around among the dancers, who bump into him and disorientate him, so that he is unable to extricate himself from the mêlée, though it is obvious that he would like to.* KOTRLÝ *has left the stage, and now he returns, carrying a large bowl which has a flame burning in it. With this in his hands, he makes his difficult way through the dancers, until at last he manages to reach the summer-house, where he puts down the bowl. As he goes, however, he sets fire to* FOUSTKA's *coat, so that a new chaotic element is added to the scene as* FOUSTKA, *his clothing on fire, runs to and fro in panic. Then, out of the summer-house where* KOTRLÝ *has placed his bowl, come thick, sulphurous fumes. The music thunders, the stage is completely obscured by smoke. As far as technically possible, the smoke invades the auditorium. After a while the music stops, the auditorium lights come on, and the audience sees that the curtain has come down in the meantime. There is a short silence, then music is heard again – this time softly and the most banal muzak. If the smoke, or the play itself, has not driven the last spectator out of the theatre, and if there is anyone left to applaud, the first to take a bow will be a fireman in uniform, with a helmet on his head and holding a fire extinguisher.*)